SCRIPTED

AN EDUCATOR'S GUIDE
TO MEDIA IN THE CLASSROOM

Paula Neidlinger   *Bruce Reicher*   *Randall Tomes*

Bruce Reicher, Paula Neidlinger, and Randall Tomes
Published by EduMatch ®
PO Box 150324, Alexandria, VA 22315
www.edumatchpublishing.com
sarah@edumatch.org.

Printed in the United States of America
First Printing 2020
First Edition 2020

ISBN: 978-1-970133-88-2

10 9 8 7 6 5 4 3 2 1

These books are available at special discounts when purchased in quantities of 10
or more for use as premiums, promotions fundraising, and educational use. For
inquiries and details, contact sarah@edumatch.org.

SCRIPTED

Scripted is a resource book for all educators providing a scope and sequence for digital media in the classroom. Each chapter provides specific resources, lessons, and classroom examples, which can be adapted to benefit your programs and needs.

It is your recipe guide to creating a successful digital media model in your school at any level. A unique perspective of this book is that we provide our classroom-proven strategies and resources based on varying teaching, geographical, and economic insights. We are confident that by sharing with you our trials and tribulations, your journey with your digital media program will be less daunting.

*Cue Cards** are located throughout the book and provide examples of documents that can be used in the classroom. All **Cue Cards** are at the end of each chapter. For updated information go to our website at www.scriptededucators.com.

Table of Contents

Chapter 1 - Shared Vision

"Leave No Rock or Stone Unturned"

Decision-Making

In the world of education, there are numerous approaches to desired outcomes. There is no "one studio in a box" for building a digital media and broadcasting program. Our intent of this book is to share and offer ideas to assist you in building or adding to your existing digital media program. Each of the examples in this book comes from our over sixty years of combined educational experience.

Creating a digital media program within a school will require numerous decisions, which will include several stakeholders in the school district. Decisions include studio space, curriculum, scheduling, equipment, funding, community involvement, and building a successful school culture.

Collaboration between the media/technology team personnel and the administration is essential for building an effective media program and/or studio. Open and honest communication with all stakeholders, which may include the principal, assistant principal, maintenance, technology, director of curriculum, and superintendent, is critical, especially in the beginning stages of a newly formed program.

Additionally, we have found it advantageous to include community members, parents, and students in our plans.

The more planning you do with each person, the more successful your studio and program will be. You will not think of everything, but many times, the smartest person in the room is the room. As your vision takes shape, all stakeholders are encouraged to contribute their ideas and ask questions. For example, the maintenance director is just as important as the superintendent when these decisions are being made, especially when power outlets are being discussed. It might be your first year in a school district, and these stakeholders will understand the culture of your community and know how to get things done in the most efficient way possible.

Studio Space

The studio space may look vastly different in each school, from a fully functional existing studio to an empty classroom. Many programs have even emerged from the back of a classroom or closet. Nevertheless, your vision must include the current available space and your goals for the program. Your program will evolve regardless of the point at which you start. It could start small with any type of media, from podcasting to a major television studio.

Where did we each begin? Our stories vary. One of us began broadcasting in a small television studio, producing weekly school announcements. In another school, the studio was no larger than a closet. That closet is now two full classrooms, which house a studio, control room, and a design lab. In another case, the radio station is set up in the back of a traditional classroom, with sound-proofing material.

An additional consideration for studio space is that it must be multifunctional. For example, it could be used for producing news broadcasts, creating green screen filming for small projects, recording podcasts, simulcasting your radio news, filming drama productions, and inviting other curricular areas to the space for special projects. Throughout the book, we will be examining how school spaces can be transformed from the simplest beginnings to full production television and radio studios.

Funding

The million-dollar question…. How much does it cost to start a digital media program? The total cost will depend on several variables. In this book, you will learn innovative ways to fund your programs, such as school budgets, grants, parent organizations, sponsorships, and community businesses and foundations. The most successful way to fund a program is by researching what resources are available in your community or state. Consider visiting other exemplary programs in your area. A rich resource is social media platforms and school websites as examples of prolific media programs. Begin creating a wish list of items that match your vision of what student achievement looks like in the digital media classroom. Throughout the book, we will share our tips on how we have successfully funded our programs. As technology teachers, we have all built production spaces over a period of time, and we know most educators will begin with the devices they have. Whether it is a laptop, tablet, cell phone, or desktop, if the device has a microphone and camera capabilities, then you are ready to begin creating media projects.

3

Program Structures

Program structure differs from school to school. In one of our programs, the studio was developed as a club, which was held before school and had less than 10 students participating. That same program today is in the school's eighth-grade schedule as a daily class, with 150 students participating each year.

In yet another example, one of our middle schools serves students through the elective process. There are now five sections a day for broadcasting. This program began as an advisory/homeroom period in its infancy. In the elementary setting, the media program is currently set up as a special area class for students in K-6, which sees over 600 students a week.

Time, student population, and daily schedule in your school may determine the structure of your program. Keep an open mind; imagine all of the possibilities for your program. We have provided three separate program structures below. Our programs are structured based on academic student needs and interests, building space, time, and program vision. Our individual visions have evolved over time, as students, parents, and community members have become advocates for the success of our programs.

Workflow (*The sequence of steps involved in moving from the beginning to the end of the working process.*)

The workflow of your program will vary in every district. We have listed below three examples of possible student and teacher workflows based on our own experiences, which could be modified in any school setting. Detailed charts and specific workflows are located in the *Cue Cards* of this chapter.

Example 1

Our first example is from an elementary perspective in which every student in the building attends the media class throughout their K-6 school experience. A live show is broadcast each day.

Teacher Workflow

Students attend the media class once every four days for a forty-five-minute class. The students learn about the three strands of communication, which include: oral, visual, and media. First through sixth-grade students become familiar with Google Apps and learn the design process. Through units of study, the students become familiar with voice work and graphic design. The goal of most projects is to get published on the school news and/or radio station. *(Cue Card 1: Scaffolding page)*

Each day, the students broadcast live to the building and the world through YouTube Live. Parents and classrooms tune into our school YouTube channel and watch the live show at 2:20 each weekday afternoon. The YouTube channel will also notify the parents when a live show is beginning.

The script is typed up each morning to provide up-to-date local weather and sports. Approximately sixty fifth and sixth graders, produce the broadcast. Each day of the week has an assigned crew. The jobs include two anchors, sports reporter, weather, attendance reporter, Tricaster operator, soundboard operator, producer, teleprompter, and three camera operators. On some days, even more students can be included in the broadcast, depending on the story they are reporting.

Student Workflow Example

The following elementary example provides a sample show schedule for schools that produce live shows and must practice during lunches, or before/after school. The tasks and position assignments can be easily adjusted for middle school and high school students and school schedules.

Sample

12:35 - During the recess or lunch period, twelve to fourteen students arrive for two run-throughs of that day's script. This usually takes twenty to thirty minutes, depending on the group. The more experienced grade levels tend to record more efficiently because they have more experience in the television studio. The goal is to introduce students to the production process at an early age so that by fifth and sixth grade, students accomplish more during rehearsal time.

During the run-throughs, anchors rehearse the script by practicing words they find difficult. They practice pronunciation and voice inflection with the assistance of the director.

The following tasks are addressed during the rehearsal:

1. Camera operators frame positions for their cameras for each segment based on the script.

2. Producers study the rundown of the script.

3. Students conduct sound checks of anchors.

4.   The teleprompter operator corrects any errors in the script and practices the pacing of the script.

5.   Switcher/engineer studies the order of the script and stories and then plans transitions between segments.

2:15 - The students arrive back to the studio and take their positions in preparation to go live. During this time, the engineer presses the streaming button to go live on YouTube. Any last-minute word pronunciations are also addressed during this time.

2:20 - An additional option for schools with radio or podcasting capabilities is to run your broadcast through the radio station at the same time. In this example, the radio record button is pressed, and the news broadcast is run into the radio soundboard to be broadcast through the radio as well. The television and radio broadcast goes live to the school and the world! Keep in mind, that if your school has streaming capabilities, a live broadcast requires a very exact rundown.

Example 2

The following example provides a sample show schedule for schools that produce live shows at the start of the day. This example requires students to arrive at the studio before school. The tasks and position assignments can be easily adjusted for elementary and high school students.

Student Workflow Example

Sample

All eighth-grade students in this example attend the broadcasting class for one marking period; there are three sections. While one group rehearses in preparation for going on air, the other two groups create and produce video features. In this particular school, an additional teacher co-teaches during production, which enables students to multi-task in separate areas. Students must produce two features per marking period.

Each group will produce fourteen shows and switch jobs once during the time they are on the air. It's important to alternate studio jobs between students throughout the marking period. All students should be proficient in every aspect of show production. Once the marking period concludes, the final group will continue production of the show until the first group of the next marking period is ready to begin their show. This method assures that a live show occurs every school day.

Students arrive fifteen minutes before the show, which is before the start of school, and review their scripts on their Chromebooks. Next, students proofread and insert comments regarding additions and deletions to the script.

An integral part of the show is having students who have already taken the class. These student producers come every day and fill in where needed. These students learn every single job throughout the year. *(Cue Card 2: Student Job Schedule)*

Teacher Workflow Example

The following example provides a sample show schedule for the teaching component from the example above. It is just as important that the teacher establishes a daily workflow for daily broadcast production. The tasks can be easily adjusted for elementary and high school students.

The teacher workflow for the live show in Example 2 above begins by updating the Google Slideshow Template that is used as the daily script for production. Show news and announcements are gathered from staff members and coaches through email. These announcements are then transferred to the Google slideshow. Other show information resources include *The New York Times* Learning section for the Day in History, the *USA Today* website for news headlines, Accuweather for our weather forecast, and a spreadsheet of student birthdays. When students arrive at school, all equipment and cues are set up for the day's show.

Example 3

In our third example, the broadcasting program is offered as an elective course at the middle school level, which meets five days a week. Mass Media 1 is a nine-week course, designed to reach at least 200 students throughout the school year, most of which are at the seventh-grade level. Mass Media 2 is an advanced semester course, composed of eighth-grade students. Media 1 is a prerequisite class. This schedule can be easily adapted to a high school daily or block schedule.

Student Workflow

Mass Media 1 is an introductory course, which explores pre-production, production, and post-production in the wide and varied fields of mass media. Students meet five days a week during a forty-five minute block of time. The major media studied are journalism, radio broadcasting, photography, social media, marketing and advertising, television and film production, photography, and videography. The entire class is built around the philosophy of student choice. Students develop writing, verbal, and directing skills through the use of computers, video and audio editing, collaboration, and live and location camera shooting, as they produce works in each of the major areas of study. Television production is centered around learning how to write and produce a feature news story for the daily/weekly announcements.

Mass Media 2 is an advanced course focused on script-writing, filmmaking, TV production, radio broadcasting, website design, advanced journalism, photography, computer graphics, social media, and marketing/advertising promotions. The class meets five days a week during a forty-five-minute block of time. Students apply advanced video techniques in the areas of pre-production, production, and post-production as they plan, produce, and edit their videos/movies and television and radio shows. Television production includes producing news segments for airing, script-writing, and production and post-production editing. The main focus is on the writing, producing, editing, and oral reporting of pertinent and current issues facing the students, community, and the world through the various vehicles of mass media.

That's a Wrap

Creating a successful digital media program necessitates time and work. Once you have the space figured out, you can begin by connecting the pieces of curriculum, hardware and software, funding, and scheduling. All media teachers take pride in possessing the grit to make all of the pieces fit. Be patient and enjoy the journey. Leave no rock or stone unturned.

 TAKE 1

> *There is no "one studio in a box" for building a digital media and broadcasting program.*

 TAKE 2

> *The vision for your program will take shape through unified decision-making by all stakeholders.*

 TAKE 3

> *Leave no rock or stone unturned, as your decisions on funding, studio space, structure, and scheduling lead you towards your vision.*

Chapter 1 Cue Cards

"Shared Vision"

Cue Card 1

Scaffolding

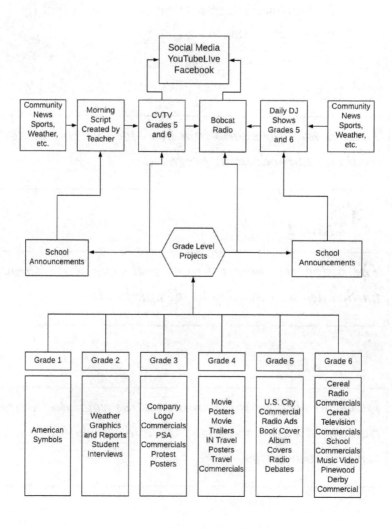

Cue Card 2

Student Job Schedule (example)

Specific descriptions of job assignments are included in the curriculum chapter.

Job Assignments

Name _____

Studio Positions	First Set	Second Set
Hosts and Feature		
Announcers/Anchors		
Sports		
Weather		
Cameras/Floor Manager		
Cameras/Floor Manager		
Control Room Positions		
Director		
Video Switcher		
Character Generator Operator		
Audio Switcher		
Music- Audio		
Computer Graphics & Recording		
Teleprompter		

Chapter 2 - Curriculum

"Media Literacy Empowers Critical Thinking"

As you begin or continue your journey developing your media classroom, you must embrace a vision for your curriculum. Ask questions such as: "How will students learn to utilize the tools of technology to create, share, and manage information? How will students facilitate the information through writing, reading, designing, creating, and producing to multiple audiences?"

There's no one path. However, it all begins with your vision. What are your objectives for your curriculum? Let your curriculum drive the technology.

The goal is to create a digital media learning environment that enables students to pursue their curiosities. Student creativity leads students to a higher level of learning. Integrating and promoting creative thinking is essential in preparing our students for their future.

Curriculum

The curriculum guides will look different in every district. We have listed below three examples of possible cross-curricular projects based on our own experiences, which can be modified in any school setting.

Detailed charts, curriculum outlines, and rubrics are located in the **Cue Cards** of this chapter.

When creating digital media curriculum, it is important to keep in mind the end product and work backward. The final product is publishing. Publishing can come in many forms, such as television shows, radio podcast/broadcast, website design, newspaper, yearbook, etc.

Steps to Creating a Unit of Study

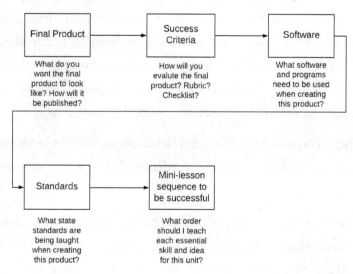

Final Product — What do you want the final product to look like? How will it be published?

Success Criteria — How will you evalute the final product? Rubric? Checklist?

Software — What software and programs need to be used when creating this product?

Standards — What state standards are being taught when creating this product?

Mini-lesson sequence to be successful — What order should I teach each essential skill and idea for this unit?

Example 1

Elementary Curriculum

The following example can be adapted to any grade and ability level. The narrative below explains how the digital media curriculum has been implemented at an elementary K-6 school.

Students meet every four days in the media classroom. Units of study introduce new programs and tools and build onto the skills they have learned in the past—the curriculum scaffolds throughout the school year in grades K-6. Students learn hardware, software, and the communication skills needed for television and radio production, which broadcasts daily throughout the school and community through our internet radio station and YouTube Live.

Example

A second grader uses a digital recorder to interview a friend for the radio. Developing interviewing skills at the second-grade level provides students the opportunity to learn how to operate digital recording tools, upload files to Google Drive, and then share files. Ultimately, the interview is broadcast on the radio or other podcasting outlets. In third grade, a student might use that same tool to capture audio for a commercial they are creating on WeVideo or other editing tools. Each year, the students in this school review what was learned the past year and are introduced to new programs to improve and design their media creations at the next level. *(Cue Card 1: Program and Tools Flowchart)*

Cross-Curricular

A perfect example of a unit of study at the fifth-grade level is a U.S. City Project. This project targets numerous standards across multiple curricula. The students are responsible for researching a city of their choice in the United States. Math standards are taught as students combine the budget and the cost to go to this city. Equations are created for calculating how much money students will need for gas if driving to their destination. The students compute the cost of the entire trip, including transportation, food, and entertainment.

Locating their city on a map also aligns with geography standards. They research flights, hotels, food, and entertainment around the city. All prices are input into a Google Sheet that is eventually included in a Google Slide presentation. Students then design a Google Slideshow and create a WeVideo commercial with the end goal of persuading viewers to visit the city, which aligns with the language arts standards. Commercials are then aired on the daily news as commercial breaks. This is one of many examples of how student-created projects can be used daily in an elementary setting, which can easily be adapted to any level. *(Cue Card 2: Media Units of Study)*

When creating an elementary studio, your goal is to involve as many students as possible when broadcasting. Students at the elementary level just want to be involved, even if it means clicking a button to move to the next screen on the teleprompter. A daily broadcast can have as many as twelve to fifteen students with a job during the broadcast. Fifth- and sixth-grade students are very capable of operating the equipment and running the studio. First through fourth-grade students should be given multiple opportunities throughout the year to work in the studio to gain experience during show production. A perfect example is a segment called "Cube Facts," where one of our fourth-grade students produces this as a weekly segment; he gives the audience an interesting fact about how to solve a Rubik's Cube.

Elementary Radio

A radio station provides students another opportunity for publishing work. Throughout the day, our students come to the radio station and broadcast live shows. Shows include topics such as fashion, sports, jokes, and even music interests. The students research artists, historical events, and current events to discuss on their live shows. School events are also announced through the radio station. The students even spin actual vinyl records on Fridays.

Radio production provides daily practice with reading fluency and voice inflection. Additionally, students become more aware of their own writing habits and practices, as they are required to research current events and news and prepare daily scripts. *(Cue Card 3: Sample Radio Script)*

Cereal Box Unit

By the sixth grade, our students have experience with numerous programs and tools, many of which are used in one unit of study. One of the flagship units is their cereal box. The box itself is something students relate to from an early age. Most of them don't realize the power of the media until they start talking about a simple cereal box. Students discuss the elements on a cereal box; by examining the covers, they discover patterns and commonalities. Before they know it, the students are using LucidChart to brainstorm what they might include on their cover and what their cereal is going to be called. Students soon move onto Lucidpress: (www.lucidpress.com), where they design their front covers. Students begin using Lucidpress in the third grade, so they are well versed in the program. Finally, they learn how to download their finished product as a JPEG or PNG for use in advertising.

Once the front and back cover of their cereal box is complete, the students are required to market their cereal on the school radio and school news. By using Soundtrap (www.soundtrap.com), the students create a radio commercial, which sometimes includes original jingles created by the students using the beats and instruments in Soundtrap. Soundtrap is a program the students become familiar with in fifth grade during the radio commercial unit of study. Once their radio commercial is complete, the students turn to creating a television commercial in WeVideo. Many students download their radio commercials in MP3 format into WeVideo to serve as their audio for their television commercials. The MP3 is also uploaded to the Vocaroo-a voice recording program: (https://vocaroo.com/). This makes it easy for listeners to hear the commercial when scanning the QR code on the cereal box. *(Cue Card 4: Cereal Box Storyboard and Rubric)*

Once their radio and television commercials are finished, they are used as commercials for radio shows the students produce daily. Google Drive has made sharing products easy for even the first graders. The television commercials serve as commercial breaks during the school's daily news program each afternoon. QR codes can also be embedded on the cereal box cover so parents and other visitors to the school building can easily scan them to see and hear student commercials. *(Cue Card 5: Cereal Box Unit Flow Chart)*

As states begin to require computer science standards, elementary students must learn the fundamentals of computer technology. Computer technology is more than teaching a student how to click a button and get to a website or type a paragraph in a document. The curriculum should be more than just going to a website and playing a game or answering questions. The curriculum should include actual creation. The students should see a reason for creation. They should always see how their creations can be published in the end. They quickly move from being consumers to producers of technology.

Example 2

Middle School Media Curriculum

The following example can be adapted to any grade and ability level. The narrative below explains how the digital media curriculum has been implemented at a middle school.

The benefits of an expansive digital media curriculum are the ability to provide a truly student-centered classroom based on choice. Mass Media classes take students on an exploration of the ever-changing world of Mass Media. This elective course is designed to introduce and develop media literacy skills, by actively engaging students in the processes and theories in media. Students explore, learn, and practice the areas of media based on their personal choices within the content of the course.

Television Curriculum

Designing an effective television curriculum cannot be done in one year. Our areas of study have evolved. Social media platforms such as Twitter and YouTube are by far one of the most efficient means of new learning for all educators. Our advice--don't recreate the wheel. There are so many brilliant educators producing quality student television every day. Contact these teachers, collaborate, and build new ideas together. Build relationships. Be open to a new mindset.

In addition to social media platforms, where can you find a quality television programming curriculum in your first year? With only a $75 annual membership, consider a membership to the Student Television Network. (https://www.studenttelevision.com/) STN provides lesson plans, digital resources, exemplary news shows, and numerous broadcasting competitions throughout the year.

The charts below reflect an overview of sample media units of study, within a television curriculum, followed by a more in-depth preview of one unit. Additionally, areas of study in both programs include appropriate leveled broadcast vocabulary, videography techniques, interview techniques, script-writing, and the importance of newsworthiness in the media industry. These units of study can easily be adapted for all grade levels and learning modalities. *(Cue Card 6: News Gathering)*

MEDIA 1

Curriculum Example

This is an example of a nine-week course structure, which meets daily for forty-five minutes. Students in this model are seventh-graders. There are occasionally first-semester eighth-grade students enrolled, as well. There are no prerequisites.

Weekly Feature Story Production: *Students develop their stories based on personal interest or current issues within the school or community setting.*	*This introductory course explores pre-production, production, and post-production in the wide and varied fields of mass media.* • *Students learn how to write and produce a feature story for the daily television announcements.*
Sports: *Students film and produce sports highlights.*	*The main focus is on the writing, producing, editing, and oral reporting of school sporting events for the television announcements.*
Extracurricular feature story and human interest production: *Students produce human interest stories.*	*The main focus is on the writing, producing, editing, and oral reporting of extracurricular events throughout the school every week.*
Mini-film production: ***One-minute films:*** *As an introduction to film production, students write, film, edit, and produce one-minute films, which are aired on our television announcements and posted to our program website. This particular project challenges students to produce a film based on what lies on the other side of a door. See the complete project details in the cue card.*	*Learning Targets - Students should be able to achieve the following targets by the end of this unit:* • *know and utilize ten camera shots and angles that can be used in film production* • *can import the film footage taken from a digital camcorder to WeVideo* • *can edit film footage, including adding title slides, music, transitions, VO's (voice-over), visual and green-*

23

(Cue Card 7: Mini-Film Door-Scene Project)	screen special effects • can export finished video as a movie and share it
Digital editing skills and videography techniques: *Students develop editing skills using WeVideo.*	*Students will develop writing, verbal, and directing skills through the use of computers, video and audio editing, collaboration, and live and location camera shooting, as they produce works in each of the major areas of study.*

MEDIA 2

Curriculum Example

This is a semester course, which meets daily for forty-five minutes.

Television production: *There are currently two, Media 2 classes. Each class produces its own show, one show a week per class. The shows are pre-recorded, uploaded to YouTube, and posted on our program website.*	*This advanced course focuses on scriptwriting, filmmaking, and television production.* ● *Students apply advanced video techniques in the areas of pre-production, production, and post-production as they plan, produce, and edit the television show.*
PSA production: *Students research a topic of interest and concern, and produce a PSA to be broadcast on the school television announcements.*	*Students create a television PSA, designed to persuade students to take a favorable action. This advanced production develops important critical thinking, literacy, and research skills.*
Commercial production: *Students travel to local community program sponsors to produce commercials.*	*Media 2 students produce 30-60 second commercials on-location in our community.* ● *Students contact the businesses, write the scripts, film, edit, and produce the finished product.* ● *These businesses sponsor our program through monetary donations and/or gift certificates to be used as giveaways on our program.*
Film production: *Students produce a five-minute film, as a culminating semester project.* **The following cue card describes, in detail, an in-depth film production**	*Media 2 students produce a five-minute feature film, as a culminating project each semester.* ● *After a short film history unit, students write original screenplays, film (both in school and on-location), edit,*

project. *(Cue Card 8: Film Project)*	*and produce their films.* • *At the conclusion of the semester, the students host their own Film Festival, which is open to the public.* • *Awards are presented in numerous categories to celebrate their accomplishments.*
Feature story and sports production: *Students produce and edit school human interest stories and sports programming.*	*The main focus is on advanced writing, producing, editing, and oral reporting of extracurricular events, sports, and human interest stories throughout the school every week.*

(Cue Card 9: Studio Positions and Show Segments)

Journalism

In Journalism, SNO Sites (https://snosites.com/) is used as the online journalism newspaper/website. It was developed as a journalism platform for schools and is a WordPress-based site, as well. The pricing is minimum, which is a consideration for many districts. Currently, there is an initial $250 set-up fee for all new sites and an annual hosting and support fee that is based on scholastic level. A journalism hosting and support plan for K-12 is currently priced at $400.00 a year. We run our entire media program through this website. It has become the voice of the school. Visitors can view our television programs, listen to our Internet school radio station, access the principal's newsletter, and check out the latest campus news, sports, and more. This is a student site written and produced by students for students. (www.ljhdigitalstorm.com)

The Yearbook class has provided an additional avenue for creativity in the program. Yearbook production incorporates photography, journalism, copy-writing, and graphic design. It provides practice with time management, prioritizing, reliability, and the responsibility of following through on tasks. This course is designed to develop students' skills in yearbook production and teach the basics of yearbook journalism, including theme, coverage, copy-writing, graphic design, photography, finance, and advertising. Students learn basic principles of yearbook production and develop skills that include writing copy, captions and headlines, digital photography, and eDesign. Yearbook Production supports students' development as writers, photographers, editors, independent users of technology, and responsible, contributing members of our school. This class is currently a semester elective class and offered to all students.

Social Media/Marketing

A marketing curriculum is most likely available through the business curriculum in a high school setting; however, at the middle school level, marketing techniques and strategies are incorporated through the study of commercial and PSA production, community sponsorships, and yearbook promotions. The goal is to expose students to as many tentacles within mass media as possible. This can't all be accomplished in your first year. Start small. Look for the possibilities within your program or classroom.

Social media curriculum will most likely differ from district to district and according to school level. Not all platforms are open and accessible to students. In our particular school, middle school students do not have access to emails, Twitter, Facebook, Instagram, or Pinterest. We have two designated classroom computers that are used by the students, with my supervision, to teach the concepts of responsible social media practices. Teaching and modeling safe and legal practices in media is a must in the digital media classroom. Consider incorporating lessons from Common Sense Media (https://www.commonsensemedia.org/)
and Google Applied Digital Skills Curriculum
(https://applieddigitalskills.withgoogle.com/s/en/home)
for an additional digital citizenship curriculum, which should be included in all digital media classes.

Radio Curriculum

Today, there are a handful of middle school radio stations, which have emerged throughout the country. Developing a progressively technology-rich curriculum, such as a school radio station, requires a growth-mindset and a proactive leader. Five years ago, through a shared vision and unique plan for students and teachers, a new class was added to our Mass Media curriculum. Student voice emerged.

Our Internet station has evolved into a primary program in all my classes. One of the greatest benefits of 21st-century technology-infused classrooms is the integration of authentic audiences. Launching a student-produced radio station has enabled our students to reach listeners worldwide with "live, local" shows produced solely by students. Most importantly, we have a global audience.

We keep listeners engaged with recorded and live programming recorded and scheduled by students during our class time, or live, during dances, lunch, sporting events, and before and after school. Students develop their radio shows based on personal interest and current school and community news and events daily.

We use Backbone Radio as the platform for our Internet Radio Station. We are members of IBS (Intercollegiate Broadcasting System) http://www.collegebroadcasters.us/content/index.html. As a member of IBS, we receive a discount on our Backbone subscription, participate in national competitions and conferences, and have access to numerous resources for school-based radio stations. Membership at the time of this writing is $125 per year.

In addition to cross-curricular opportunities for all students within the school building, radio broadcasting possibilities include the following examples:

- *Producing radio commercials for community sponsors.*

- *Producing PSAs.*

- *Producing radio promotions for marketing purposes.*

- *Broadcasting play-by-play sporting events and special school events, such as dances, plays, or music concerts.*

- *Broadcasting on-location community special events.*

- *Hosting a radio day twice a year.*

- *Hosting local civic organizations in-studio podcasts and radio shows.*

- *Hosting Vinyl Fridays, which is student-produced.*

(Cue Card 10: Royalty-Free Music Resource)

Radio Project Example

"Once in A Fairy Tale" is a project which combines both radio and television.

Challenge

Taking on the role of a reporter for the 6:00 p.m. news, students choose a classic fairy tale and create a television "breaking news" story about the characters and events. The report is based on the conflict of the story and incorporates the characters and events in the actual fairy tale. Next, the story is produced in the studio, providing Media 1 students an opportunity to learn about studio production. Students edit their news stories through WeVideo.

After a brief study of early radio production, students transform the television scripts by telling the story through radio using sound effects and voices of the characters. Writing for radio is much different than television. The final scripts must paint a picture in the audience's mind, create action through dialogue, utilize natural and digital sound effects, create believable characters, and must include precise and clear language.

Students have several choices of scripts.

a.   Expand the original TV script-keep as a news story but with additional facts.

b.   Write a modern twist on the story.

c.   Produce one of the actual versions of the story using music, sound effects, and the voices of the characters.

d.   Produce a series of short news stories using several news scripts.

Students create an intro to the radio show, including the name, sponsor, and intro music (ex: "Welcome to the Storm Radio Drama Hour sponsored by Tornado Crispies, the twisty, toasty, honey-coated cereal.")

Example 3

Media Production Class for Live Show

The following example can be adapted to any grade and ability level. The narrative below explains how digital media curriculum has been implemented at a middle school.

The following production class example is based on another possible schedule scenario. The curriculum has two distinct parts. The first element is learning all the jobs needed to produce a live show. The second part is to create all the content for the show. The class meets twenty-two times during a marking period for forty-eight minutes. The students produce a live show every day. The show is streamed throughout the school, and the recording is posted on the school website. The charts below detail both sections of the class.

Video Production

Create 30 second opening for the show	This lesson is used as an introduction to WeVideo tools.
	• The opening includes text, video, and music of all elements of the show made in WeVideo.
	• Elements include: pledge, day in history, weather, interviews, features, guess the teacher, announcements, and sports.
	• The openings are rotated daily.

Bumpers for show: (teases or transitions connecting segments)	All bumpers include text, video, graphics, and music. Types of bumpers "include:" • Sports • Weather • Feature
Feature story for the show *(Cue Card 11: Feature Story Checklist)*	Each group of students will produce two stories per marking period which includes: • Brainstorm ideas • Research ideas and gather facts for opening and questions • Write opening voice-over, questions, and closing • Record voice-overs • Record stand-up using green-screen • Record interviews • Import and edit footage • Add titles • Add cutaways or picture-in-picture for every clip
Pledge of Allegiance	Create a pledge with video and images from national landmarks: • Find images and video from WeVideo essential collection • Record the students saying the pledge for voice-over
Digital Citizenship Public Service Announcements	Create a WeVideo PSA using the following tools: • Research topics in Brainpop.com • Create a Google Doc with 10 facts about Digital Citizenship • These facts become text boxes in

	video and are matched up with video and still clips • Add music from WeVideo for effect

Live Show Classes (4 of the 22 classes)

Sign up for broadcasting jobs	• Students choose what type of job they would like to do • Students take a tour of the studio
Rehearsals	• Teach each individual job • Practice with the existing script • Go through all rundowns • As students switch jobs during the marking period, they train each other

Another recipe for success in the media classroom is the addition of the Google Education Applied Digital Skills curriculum. The curriculum is video-driven and allows students to move at their own pace through interactive learning. The project-based digital skills curriculum includes lessons in digital collaboration and publishing, coding, data analysis, effective communication and research skills, and writing strategies for the media classroom.

(https://applieddigitalskills.withgoogle.com/s/en/home)

Assessment - Rubrics

The curriculum is a fluid document that is always changing and improving every day. The more time you invest in planning out your lessons, the better results you will achieve. It's important to understand that producing media takes time to master. Additionally, in most cases, you will be modeling for students. Make sure you have enough time in your plan for students to produce their projects. For example, in middle school, it might take students up to four weeks to produce a two to three-minute video feature, depending on the flexibility of the schedule. Set high expectations. Utilize exemplary productions as the standard. It will take the students time to create their masterpiece.

The following Cue Cards provide examples of rubrics used for assessment in our classes. *(Cue Card 12: Media Rubrics)*

That's a Wrap

Develop a vision based on the standards in your state and corporation. Construct the steps and lessons you will need to facilitate the learning. As you have discovered in this chapter, the digital media curriculum is an expansive concept. Our vision for the digital media classroom is to foster student development of critical thinking and literacy skills to become more informed, reflective, and engaged participants in society.

 TAKE 1

Embrace a concept for your curriculum; there's more than one path.

 TAKE 2

Create digital media opportunities to perpetuate student curiosities.

 TAKE 3

Integrate and promote creative thinking.

Chapter 2 Cue Cards

"Curriculum"

Cue Card 1

Media Curriculum

Programs Used in Media Curriculum

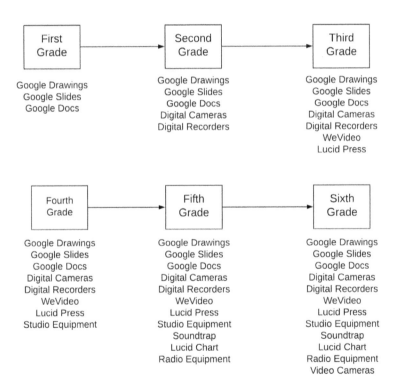

Cue Card 2

Curriculum Example

Elementary School Media Curriculum

The following is a summary of the units of study for each grade level. Most of the units of study allow for the students to publish their work through our school television studio (CVTV) or Backbone Radio (Bobcat Radio). The goal is to have continuous rotation of student work through our daily news program or our student-run radio shows. These are possible units of study for your elementary school, middle school, or high school, as these units can all be tailored to align with your state standards.

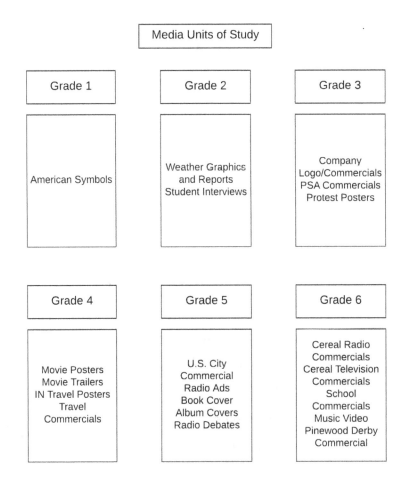

Grade 2 Curriculum

UNIT OF STUDY: Photography Book

VISUAL COMMUNICATION

Focus on taking digital pictures and uploading to Google Drive

TECHNOLOGY USED: Google Drive, Google Slides, cameras, SD cards, and USB cords

STUDENT OBJECTIVE: Students will take photos using digital cameras, upload them to a Google Drive, and create a ten slide Google Slide Show.

UNIT OF STUDY: What's news?

MEDIA LITERACY: Media has its own language

TECHNOLOGY: Docs, newspaper templates online

UNIT OF STUDY: Weather reporting

THEME: Communicators ask questions, research, share

ORAL COMMUNICATION: Focus on eye contact

TECHNOLOGY USED: Internet research, Google Slides, Television Studio

STUDENT OBJECTIVE: Students will create a weather temperature chart using Google Slides, share the chart with the teacher, and present the weather on the school news.

UNIT OF STUDY: Radio interviews

THEME: Communicators ask questions, research, share

ORAL COMMUNICATIONS: Focus on eye contact. Determine if eye contact is the best focus for this one and how to integrate it

TECHNOLOGY USED: Digital recorders, Google Drive, Backbone Radio, Google Docs

STUDENT OBJECTIVE: Students will type in ten questions to ask a friend and use the digital recorders to record an interview with a friend. Students will upload the finished interview to their Google Drive and share it with the teacher to put on the school radio.

UNIT OF STUDY: Digital timeline

RESEARCH: Focus on events and organizing sequentially online

TECHNOLOGY: Google Slides

SKILLS: Organizing events visually

STUDENT OBJECTIVE: Students will create a timeline of their life on Google Slides and convert the slide to JPEG format.

Grade 3 Curriculum

UNIT OF STUDY: Community signs: logos and slogans

THEME: Communicators connect to their community through a variety of ways

VISUAL COMMUNICATION: Focus on font, tips for logos, and slogans

TECHNOLOGY USED: Google Slides, Flamingtext

STUDENT OBJECTIVE: Students will create a made-up company and design a logo for that company on Google Slides. Students will save the logo as a JPEG and share it with their teacher.

UNIT OF STUDY: Commercials

THEME: Communicators connect to their community through a variety of ways

MEDIA LITERACY: Focus media have embedded values

TECHNOLOGY USED: Digital Recorders, WeVideo, Google Drive, Google Slides

STUDENT OBJECTIVE: Students will create a thirty-second commercial with music and narration for their made-up company in WeVideo. Students will upload audio recordings to their Google Drive and then WeVideo.

UNIT OF STUDY: Public Service Announcements

THEME: Communicators connect to their community through a variety of ways

ORAL COMMUNICATION: Focus on font/poise

TECHNOLOGY USED: Digital Recorders, WeVideo, Google Drive, Google Slides

STUDENT OBJECTIVE: Students will research a cause and create a one-minute Public Service Announcement in WeVideo.

UNIT OF STUDY: Protest signs

THEME: Communicators connect to their community through a variety of ways

VISUAL COMMUNICATION: Focus on colors and emotions

TECHNOLOGY USED: Lucidpress, Google Drive

STUDENT OBJECTIVE: Students will create a protest poster in Lucidpress and save it as a JPEG to their Google Drive.

Grade 4 Curriculum

UNIT OF STUDY: Writing Opinion Pieces

THEME: Communicators read and write like authors

WRITTEN COMMUNICATION: Focus on point of view

TECHNOLOGY USED: Google Docs, Website authors reading kids' reviews

STUDENT OBJECTIVE: Students will write a movie and share it on the school news.

UNIT OF STUDY: Movie Poster

THEME: Communicators persuade through imagery

VISUAL COMMUNICATION: Focus on context, if students had to make a presentation to their class using the poster as a prop

TECHNOLOGY USED: Lucidpress, Flamingtext

STUDENT OBJECTIVE: Students will use Lucidpress to create a movie poster for a movie they would like to make someday. Students will convert the file to a JPEG when finished.

UNIT OF STUDY: Movie Trailers

THEME: Communicators persuade through imagery

VISUAL COMMUNICATION: Important Content

TECHNOLOGY USED: WeVideo, Google Drive, Lucidpress, Digital Cameras, Digital Recorders

STUDENT OBJECTIVE: Students will use WeVideo to create a sixty-second movie trailer. Students will include their movie poster in the trailer.

UNIT OF STUDY: What is news? Why does news matter?

THEME: Communicators read and write like authors/reporters

MEDIA LITERACY: Messages are constructed, using creative language with its own rules

TECHNOLOGY USED: Digital databases, Google Docs, Lucidpress

STUDENT OBJECTIVE: Students will use Lucidpress to create one page of a classroom newspaper.

UNIT OF STUDY: Credible sources/citations

THEME: Communicators read, write, and research like authors

RESEARCH: Focus on how to determine credibility

TECHNOLOGY USED: Internet/Google Docs

STUDENT OBJECTIVE: Students will include direct quotations in their newspaper story page from an interview and/or research.

UNIT OF STUDY: Indiana posters/Commercials

THEME: Communicators persuade through imagery

VISUAL COMMUNICATION: Focus on context

TECHNOLOGY USED: Lucidpress, Google Drive, Flamingtext, WeVideo

STUDENT OBJECTIVE: Students will use Lucidpress to create a travel poster for a destination in Indiana. Students will create a commercial for their destination in Indiana.

UNIT OF STUDY: Photography

THEME: Communicators persuade through imagery

VISUAL COMMUNICATION: Focus on context

TECHNOLOGY USED: Digital cameras, Google Slides

STUDENT OBJECTIVE: Students will use digital cameras to take different types of shots studied in class around the school. Students will create a Google Slides portfolio to share their photos.

UNIT OF STUDY: News broadcast

THEME: Communicators read and write like authors

MEDIA LITERACY: Messages are constructed, uses creative language with its own rules

TECHNOLOGY USED: TV studio

STUDENT OBJECTIVE: Students will work in groups of 10-12 to put on a news show for the school.

Grade 5 Curriculum

UNIT OF STUDY: Getting to Know Me

THEME: Communication through mass media

VISUAL COMMUNICATION: Focus on tone and perspective

TECHNOLOGY USED: Google Slides

STUDENT OBJECTIVE: Students will design a ten-slide Google Slides presentation introducing themselves to the class.

UNIT OF STUDY: Trip to a U.S. City

THEME: Communication through mass media

VISUAL COMMUNICATION: Focus on information design and communication

TECHNOLOGY USED: Google Search, Google Slides, Google Sheets, WeVideo

Targets: Fifth Grade Trip Targets

STUDENT OBJECTIVE: Students will create a slideshow persuading the audience to visit one U.S. city. Students will research and link each slide to a main slide. Students will create a 60-second commercial in WeVideo to persuade their audience to visit their city. Students will present a budget for the trip.

UNIT OF STUDY: Using Wikipedia

THEME: Communication through mass media

RESEARCH: Spotting errors, reliable sources

TECHNOLOGY USED: Wikipedia and online sources

STUDENT OBJECTIVE: Students will support Wiki research with other reliable websites (.org .gov).

UNIT OF STUDY: Media literacy and advertisements

THEME: Communication through mass media

MEDIA LITERACY: Media have embedded values (What lifestyle, values, and points of view are represented or omitted from this message?)

TECHNOLOGY USED: Soundtrap, Backbone Radio

STUDENT OBJECTIVE: Students will use Soundtrap to create a thirty-second radio commercial advertising a product of their choice.

UNIT OF STUDY: Photography

THEME: Communication through mass media

VISUAL COMMUNICATION: Focus on perspective and the ethics of editing photos

TECHNOLOGY USED: Pixlr, Google Slides, Lucidpress

STUDENT OBJECTIVE: Students will learn how to edit themselves into a destination picture of their choice.

UNIT OF STUDY: Radio

THEME: Mass media communications

ORAL COMMUNICATION: Focus on speed, content and adding ambient sound

TECHNOLOGY USED: Internet sources, audio recorders, sound cutting program

STUDENT OBJECTIVE: Students will produce their own radio show, including songs, commercials, and commentary.

UNIT OF STUDY: Debates

THEME: Communication and points of view

ORAL COMMUNICATION: Focus on rules of debate and an articulate presentation

TECHNOLOGY USED: TV studio

STUDENT OBJECTIVE: Students will research a debate topic and present their side to the class.

UNIT OF STUDY: Record Cover

THEME: Communicators persuade through imagery

VISUAL COMMUNICATION: Important Content

TECHNOLOGY USED: Lucidpress, Flamingtext, Google Drive, Pixlr

STUDENT OBJECTIVE: Students will re-create a record cover for an old 45 rpm record.

UNIT OF STUDY: Book Cover

THEME: Communicators persuade through imagery

VISUAL COMMUNICATION: Imagery can persuade

TECHNOLOGY USED: Lucidpress, Google Drive

STUDENT OBJECTIVE: Students will create a new cover for their favorite book using Lucidpress. Students will present the cover and a short book review as a segment on the school news using WeVideo to create.

Grade 6 Curriculum

UNIT OF STUDY: Cereal Box

THEME: Communication connects across the world

ORAL COMMUNICATION: Focus on gestures and props

MEDIA LITERACY: Interpretation, personal statement about food

TECHNOLOGY USED: POV film clips, Lucidpress

STUDENT OBJECTIVE: Students will create a new cereal box using Lucidpress.

UNIT OF STUDY: Cereal Box Advertisement

THEME: Product design persuades buyers

RESEARCH: What persuades buyers to purchase a product.

TECHNOLOGY USED: Google, Lucidpress, Flamingtext, WeVideo

VISUAL COMMUNICATION: Focus on negative space and emphasis

TARGETS: Sixth Grade Cereal Box Targets

STUDENT OBJECTIVE: Students will create a thirty-second radio commercial for their cereal using Soundtrap. Students will create a thirty-second television commercial for their cereal using WeVideo.

UNIT OF STUDY: International brochure

THEME: Communication connects across the world

VISUAL COMMUNICATION: Focus on negative space and emphasis

ORAL COMMUNICATION: Focus on six concepts and using multimedia component

TECHNOLOGY USED: Citing sources, QR codes, WeVideo, YouTube

STUDENT OBJECTIVE: Students will create a brochure on a country of their choice using Lucidpress. Students will create a sixty-second commercial advertising their country using WeVideo. Students will upload their commercials to YouTube. Students will create a QR code that links to their commercial on YouTube.

UNIT OF STUDY: Film study

THEME: Communication connects across the world

VISUAL COMMUNICATION: Focus on the use of negative space and film techniques

MEDIA LITERACY: Audience analysis

TECHNOLOGY USED: Digital Video Cameras, WeVideo, Digital Recorders, Google, Green Screen, Panzoid

STUDENT OBJECTIVE: Students will create a short news segment using WeVideo. Students will code on Panzoid to create the introduction of their commercial. (Example: Estimation of the Week, iSpy video, short interviews)

UNIT OF STUDY: Music video

THEME: Communication connects across the world

MEDIA LITERACY: Focus on analysis of lyrics, visual communication

TECHNOLOGY USED: Lucidcharts (storyboarding), WeVideo, YouTube videos, Sony Video Cameras, Google Drive

STUDENT OBJECTIVE: Students will work in small groups to re-create a music video from the 60s, 70s, or 80s. Students will edit in WeVideo.

UNIT OF STUDY: Cyberbullying

THEME: Communication connects across the world

MEDIA LITERACY: Social messages organized to gain power (Key question: Why was this message sent?) self-reflection, district policy

TECHNOLOGY USED: WeVideo, Lucidcharts (storyboarding)

STUDENT OBJECTIVE: Students will create a thirty-second anti-bullying commercial.

UNIT OF STUDY: Roller Coaster

THEME: Communication through mass media

VISUAL COMMUNICATION: Point-of-view

TECHNOLOGY USED: YouTube, WeVideo, Green screen, television studio, Tri-caster

STUDENT OBJECTIVE: Students will create a point-of-view ride of a rollercoaster of their choice. Students will record POV using the TriCaster and YouTube and edit on WeVideo.

UNIT OF STUDY: Advertising Pinewood Derby Team

THEME: Communication connects across the world

MEDIA LITERACY: Most media messages are organized to gain profit and/or power (Why was this message sent?)

TECHNOLOGY USED: WeVideo, Digital Cameras, Lucidpress, Google Docs, Soundtrap, Google Sites

STUDENT OBJECTIVE: Students will write a business letter to a local company asking permission to put their logo on their pinewood derby car. Students will create an advertisement poster for their car team. Students will create a radio commercial for the pinewood derby. Students will use WeVideo to create a thirty-second commercial to advertise their car sponsor. Students will create a Google Site for their team.

Cue Card 3

Vinyl Friday Script Sheet

Welcome back to _____ Radio... and this Vinyl Friday! For the next twenty minutes, we will be your radio DJs for _____(Today's Date). All music today will be played on an old Califone Record Player. This is the true analog sound for your ears and mine. Today we will be listening to the sounds of _____(Artist's Name)

(Please share three facts about your artist:)

_____

_____

_____

For _____ first song we have:

_____

(Place the Needle on the record and play song #1)

We hope you are enjoying our Vinyl Friday...I'm _____ playing some of the hits of _____.

Our next song by _____ is

_____

(Provide one or two facts about the song you are about to play)

_____

_____

_____

And here is

_____

(Play song #2)

You are listening to Vinyl Friday.

Next, we have

_____

(Play song #3)

That was _____ (song #3 name)

(Provide a fact about song #3)

_____

_____

I hope you have enjoyed listening to

_____.

Thank you for listening to _____Radio on this Vinyl Friday. I am _____ and I have enjoyed bringing you the sweet sounds of Vinyl records by _____ (artist name)

To end Vinyl Friday we are going to break out one of (his, her, their) greatest hits.

(Provide a little background information on the last song you are going to play. What year was it made? Where was it recorded? What number did it climb to on the Billboard Charts?)

_____

_____

_____

_____

Have a great Friday! Here is _____ (song #4)

(Play song #4)

Cue Card 4

Cereal Box Example

Cereal Box Commercial Rubric					
Student Name_____ Commercial Name_____					
CATEGORY	4	3	2	1	Total
Voice consistency	Voice quality is clear and consistently audible throughout the presentation.	Voice quality is clear and consistently audible throughout the majority (85-95%) of the presentation.	Voice quality is clear and consistently audible through some (70-84%) of the presentation.	Voice quality needs more attention.	
Soundtrack emotion	Music stirs a rich emotional response that matches the theme of the cereal.	Music stirs a rich emotional response that somewhat matches the theme of the cereal.	Music is ok, and not distracting, but it does not add much to the theme of the cereal.	Music is distracting, inappropriate, or was not used.	

Images	Images create a distinct atmosphere or tone that matches different parts of the story. The images may communicate symbolism and/or metaphors.	Images create an atmosphere or tone that matches some parts of the story. The images may communicate symbolism and/or metaphors.	An attempt was made to use images to create an atmosphere/tone but it needed more work. Image choice is logical.	Little or no attempt to use images to create an appropriate atmosphere/tone.	
Duration of presentation	Length of presentation was thirty seconds or more.	Length of presentation was at least twenty-five seconds.	Length of presentation was at least twenty seconds.	Presentation was less than twenty seconds.	
Economy	The commercial is told with exactly the right amount of detail throughout. It does not seem too short nor does it seem too long.	The commercial composition is typically good, though it seems to drag somewhat OR need slightly more detail in one or two sections.	The commercial seems to need more editing. It is noticeably too long or too short in more than one section.	The commercial needs extensive editing. It is too long or too short to be interesting.	
Comments:				Total Points:	
				Letter Grade:	

Cue Card 5

Cereal Box Flowchart

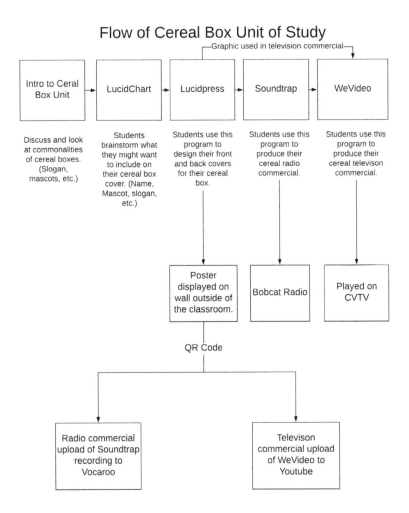

Flow of Cereal Box Unit of Study

Cue Card 6

Infographic of Possible News Sites

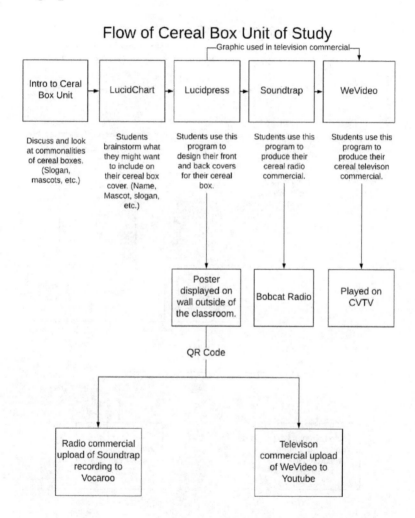

This infographic was created using Canva. It is housed on our class home page, as a news gathering resource tool. Each of the (example) news sites are linked, which provides students quick access to up-to-date "News They Can Use," while preparing their scripts or feature stories. Adjust the sites needed according to your local news sites.

Cue Card 7

Recreate One-Minute Door Scene

Media 1: Introduction to Film

Production

This project introduces Media 1 students to film production. This project can be adapted in numerous ways. It serves as a springboard to advanced film production at the Media 2 level.

The Scenario

Each team produces a one-minute scene using the scenario below. Ironically, no one door scene has ever been the same.

(This scene is an example of one possibility)

Scene: A person is about to open a door. (Students can use any door in the building)

- The person hears a sound and becomes mildly concerned. The sound could be on either side of the door. Students must decide if it's a sound they're trying to reach or get away from.
- The person finds the door locked and searches for his or her keys. Students must use keys as a prop for this project.
- The person hears the sound again and becomes visibly apprehensive (anxious & fearful). As the filmmaker, the goal is to build tension and growing panic, using any visual element or device that will accomplish the goal.
- The film closes with the person finally opening the door and getting to the other side safely. Students must communicate to the audience the character's feeling of relief and safety. At

this point, students may incorporate a cliffhanger, as an essence of suspense.

Parameters (teams of two only)

- Neither the character nor the audience **ever** sees the source of the sound.

  o At least **10** different shot types/angles must be used.

  o **Draw and/or describe these shots using a storyboard** before filming begins. (An example of the storyboard used is located below.)

  o The film can have only **one actor.**

  o The film is **one minute** in length.

  o The entire film must take place within **five feet of either side of the door.**

Cue Card 8

Film Festival

Media 2

Film production is another opportunity for activating student voice and creativity in a media classroom. In this example, Media 1 students learn the basics of film production by producing a one-minute door scene, as described above. In Media 2, students produce a five-minute film, which is the culminating project of the semester. A film festival is held both semesters, celebrating student accomplishments. The feature films are then submitted to the Student Television Network, as part of their Film Excellence competition. This is an option, but submitting student work to additional outlets provides opportunities for global exposure and recognition.

In this project, students choose their own groups of four to six. The project is produced over a nine-week period of time, which is simultaneously being produced during regularly scheduled television and radio broadcasting shows. Students write their original screenplay, create their storyboard, shoot the film both inside and outside of the school day, edit, produce, and market their films. *(example of storyboard below)* There are several options when creating storyboards. This example assists students in creating cohesive storylines by aligning the storyboard and plot map.

1. Opening Scene Setting

_____

_____

_____

shot_____

2. Rising Action   **3. Rising Action**   **4. Rising Action**

shot_____   shot_____   shot_____

5. Rising Action   **6. Rising Action**   **7. Rising Action**

_____   _____   _____

_____   _____   _____

_____   _____   _____

shot_____   shot_____   shot_____

8. Climax   **9. Falling Action**   **10. Resolution**

shot_____ shot_____ shot_____

Judges are secured outside of the school district, to ensure fairness and impartiality. After the unit, a film festival is held, premiering all of the films. Students are recognized for their accomplishments and awarded trophies accordingly, during an awards ceremony after the films have been presented.

Learning Targets

- *I know a number of different shots and angles that can be used when filming.*

- *I can use a number of different shots and angles when actually taking film footage.*

- *I can import the film footage I have taken from a digital camcorder to WeVideo.*

- *I can edit my film footage, including adding title slides, music, and transitions.*

- *I can export my finished video as a movie, and share it.*

General Judging Guidelines

The following guidelines are used as the basis for the student competition at the local level.

Contest entries are judged by industry professionals. It's beneficial to secure judges outside of our school district, so that judging is fair and impartial. Additionally, films are submitted to The Student Television Network, as part of their Film Excellence Competition.

- **Camera/Direction**: Do the visuals tell the story? Are shots steady, focused, and well composed?

- **Lighting**: Are the visuals crisp and clear? Did the videographer avoid poor lighting situations?
- **Audio**: Are the sounds and voice tracks clean and clear? Are the soundbites clean and clear?
- **Nat Sound**: Did the story begin with great natural sound? Are there natural sound moments incorporated into the story?
- **Editing**: Does the editing distract away from the story? Are the sequences and transitions smooth?
- **Drama/Human Interest**: Did the story appeal to the emotions? Was the story compelling?
- **Storytelling/Script**: Does the story have good structure and flow?
- **Creativity**: Is the idea original or presented in an original manner?
- **Complexity**: Does the video have a high production value?
- **Talent/Acting/Performance**: Did the talent perform in an appropriate manner for the production?
- **Graphics/Effects**: Did the graphics/effects add to the production?
- **Followed Directions**: Did the entry meet the film competition objectives?

Film Award Categories

All films are entered in the categories listed below. The films are judged by personnel outside of the school district. Awards are announced at the conclusion of the film festival in each of the categories listed below. Trophies are presented to each member of the winning films.

Our categories include:

* BEST FILM

* BEST FILM EDITING

* BEST CINEMATOGRAPHY

* BEST VISUAL EFFECTS

* BEST SOUND EDITING

* BEST SCREENPLAY

* BEST MARKETING DIRECTOR

* BEST DIRECTOR

* BEST ACTOR AND BEST ACTRESS IN A LEADING ROLE

* BEST SUPPORTING ACTOR AND ACTRESS

Marketing

Each group is responsible for marketing their film before film release.

1. Trailer

Each team produces a trailer for their film. This is produced once the final film production is completed. The trailer theme must be appropriate based on film genre. The trailers are shown on the school television show/announcements and uploaded to the school program website.

The main purpose of a trailer is to encourage people to want to see the film. The trailer, along with other marketing materials, previews what the film offers.

2. Social Media

Students use classroom computers to tweet and post their trailers and promos for their films.

3. Digital Poster

Students create digital posters using Canva. The posters are displayed throughout the school, as well as our program website and on social media.

The poster includes the following information:

* *Title*

* *Tagline*

* *Picture that reflects the film*

* *Date of festival*

* *Time*

* *Location*

* *Additional information: film production team; stars; reviews; etc.*

Exemplary examples are provided for students.

4. Radio Promo

Each group produces a thirty-second radio/podcast promo for their film. The promo includes:

* Name of film

* Plot of film

* Date of film

* Where and when film will be debuted

5. Invitations

Invitations are printed in advance and distributed to each film team. Each film team student signs and hand delivers invitations for the film festival to teachers, parents, families, and at least one community member. All sponsors receive an invitation by mail.

Cue Card 9

Consider posting all job responsibilities on the bulletin board in the control room or classroom, as a checklist for all studio positions during production.

Television Studio Positions

Listed below are examples of possible television studio positions and segments within a show that could be incorporated once the studio has evolved. These positions might not be necessary in the infancy of your program. Students have a choice and a voice in the position and an opportunity to experience multiple jobs throughout the class duration. It is advantageous for students to learn as many positions as possible, especially in the control room.

Anchor On-Air Personality

Practice, practice, practice. Anchors must practice reading their scripts beforehand. As an anchor, students are expected to take pride in their appearance. We provide matching polo shirts for all anchors, which have been purchased through community sponsorships. Students write their scripts for each show using information that has been submitted by teachers and coaches. A "Submit News Here" form is linked on the student website.

Student anchors must rehearse their scripts in advance to deliver the news in a professional, engaging way. Finally, it's important to incorporate as many anchor positions as possible, so that multiple students have experience in front of the camera. Listed below are possible multiple anchor segments within a show broadcast:

- Introduction to show
- Campus News
- World News
- Weather
- Sports
- Coach's Couch
- Hot Seat
- Special Segments
- Minute-to-Win It
- Guess the Teacher
- Student Spotlight
- National Day
- This Week/Day in History
- Community Couch
- Lunch, Birthdays, Attendance
- Feature Stories
- Outro, Quote of the Day

Director

The director is the key communicator between the control room and floor studio. The Student Director is responsible for the flow of the show. During production, the director communicates through wireless headsets to all studio personnel. Additionally, it is recommended that the student director be proficient and knowledgeable on all control room equipment.

Engineer

The student engineer operates the software-driven video production technology. It is beneficial to have an extra computer/script for the engineer to refer to during production. All graphics/videos/music should be uploaded before production. Transitions and informational headlines/subtitles/captions should be added in advance. The engineer and director need to work together throughout the production process.

Floor Manager

The floor manager communicates between the director and the anchor(s). A wireless intercom system works best for live television production. Additionally, the floor manager is responsible for making sure that the scripts have been added to the master script and that graphics and videos have been given to the engineer.

Camera Operator/Studio Manager

The Camera Operator follows the direction of the director and adjusts the cameras in multi and single camera operational conditions. These positions can be combined depending on the number of students you have available and the size of your studio space. This student is responsible for setting up the studio before the show and shutting all equipment down after production. Additionally, this student adjusts set furniture and microphones as needed during the show.

Audio/Sound Technician

The audio/sound technician operates the sound levels from the various audio inputs in the control room. This is an extremely important job. The student must get set up and check the microphones before each segment, so that adjustments can be made if needed. The audio technician should confirm that all soundtracks/music/jingles/etc. are added to the video recording system with the assistance of the engineer. Consider labeling the various audio cables coming into the audio board. This simple trick alleviates possible mistakes during a production.

Teleprompter

The teleprompter technician is responsible for setting up the script on the teleprompter program before production. They should work alongside the Floor Manager and ensure the script is written correctly. The anchors and teleprompter technician must practice beforehand to adjust the script speed and set accordingly. This is sometimes one of the most difficult tasks during production. A teleprompter can be created in many simple, inexpensive ways such as a computer, laptop, tablet, or an old television monitor. In place of expensive software, Google Slides, Microsoft PowerPoint, or a free app could be used.

Graphics

Although not required, consider assigning a Graphics Director/Coordinator. This student confirms all images are copyright-free and labeled for reuse if they are not photos taken by the production students. Consider offering this student creative design opportunities throughout the production process, from video creation of intros and outros, transitions, logos, and even set design.

There are numerous methods of assigning studio positions. Auditions can be held for anchor positions either through a live studio process or a student-produced audition videotape. A written application can be incorporated, which reinforces writing standards. Once positions have been assigned, consider rotating jobs frequently, providing numerous opportunities for all students.

Example of Studio Position Assignment Spreadsheet

Assignments can be posted through a spreadsheet or posted on a bulletin board for easy access.

	Monday	Tuesday	Wednesday	Thursday	Friday
Teacher					
Anchor 1					
Anchor 2					
Sports					
Weather					
Tech Director					
Director					

Camera 1					
Camera 2					
Teleprompter					
Sound					
Attendance					
Manager					

Cue Card 10

Music Infographic

MOST REQUESTED
ROYALTY FREE MUSIC SITES

01 **INC►MPETECH**

02 **ZAPSPLAT**

03 ►**YouTube**

04 **dig cc mixter**

05 ⌁**freesound**

CONTENT CREATOR

panzoid

This music infographic was created using Canva. It is housed on my class home page, as a creative commons music resource tool. Each of the music sites is linked, which provides students quick access to royalty-free music sites for radio and television production. Soundtrap, Audacity, and GarageBand, also provide students with creative alternatives to music resources.

Cue Card 11

Feature Checklist

This checklist is a sample checklist, which can be adapted for all feature story productions.

Ordered Checklist for feature stories

❏ Brainstorm five ideas for features (school appropriate)

❏ Research an angle for your feature

❏ Write a well-written open, middle, and closing in Google Docs

❏ Include media (video or pictures for your opening)

❏ Plan who you are interviewing and include open-ended questions for each person (review the difference between open-ended and close-ended questions)

❏ Record voice over

❏ Record in front of the green screen

❏ Interview three to four experts

❏ Incorporate titles of everyone you interview

❏ Test audio levels

❏ Shoot in thirds (Review Rule of Thirds- See Glossary)

❏ Crop every video clip so there is no headroom (Review Camera Composition Criteria)

❏   Use cutaways and picture-in-picture

❏   Include B-roll in your feature (Review the difference between A-roll and B-roll- See Glossary)

❏   Include music track(s)

❏   Collaborate with teacher

Cue Card 12

Rubric

The following pages provide a sample rubric idea for any media project.

VIDEO or AUDIO PROJECT

CONTENT	1	2	3
Overall effectiveness of video	Video was not visually interesting. Did not show much imagination. Did not convey information or a compelling message.	Video was effective or appealing, but not both.	Video was effective, informative, and appealing.
Effectiveness of introduction	Viewer had no reason to keep watching.	Viewer was fairly well interested in the introduction.	Viewer was hooked from the beginning of the video and kept interest throughout.
Project clarity	Many elements of the video were irrelevant to the overall message. Viewer was not sure what the message was.	Most elements of the video were relevant to the overall theme. Events and messages were mostly clear and in order.	All elements of the video were relevant to the overall theme. Events and messages were in a clear and sensible order.
Completion of assignment	Few elements of the assignment were addressed satisfactorily.	Most of the elements of the assignment were addressed satisfactorily.	All elements of the assignment were addressed satisfactorily.
Indication of thinking and learning	There was little indication of imagination, creativity, research, and	Video showed a basic command of the subject, but lacked creativity and thoughtfulness.	Video showed creativity, motivation, and critical thinking. The presenters clearly had an

	thoughtfulness in the video.		understanding of the topic and did the necessary research.
MEDIA	1	2	3
Good audio and visual continuity	Transitions from shot to shot were choppy. Effects were either missing or excessive. Sound was cut-off and/or inconsistent.	Video sometimes moved smoothly from shot to shot. Use of effects is not always worthwhile. Sound was well-placed and reasonably consistent.	Video moved smoothly from shot to shot. Good but not excessive use of effects. Sound was well-placed and consistent.
Use of media resources (music, text, voice-overs, pictures, video)	Little use was made of media resources. Video would have benefited from more diverse media.	Media resources were present but not always balanced. Most media was relevant to the purpose of the video.	Media resources were well-balanced. All media was relevant to the purpose of the video. All available resources were used effectively.

GROUP SKILLS	1	2	3
Plan with a focus statement, script, and storyboard	Group did not complete a plan before filming and editing.	Group completed a plan that was mostly followed during the project.	Group completed a well-organized plan that was successfully followed during the project.
Group participation	Work was dominated by individual(s).	Most of the group had a meaningful role in the project.	All members of the group had an equal and meaningful role in all aspects of the project.
Group interaction	Group decisions were either never made or were dominated by individual(s).	Group had some problems making decisions by consensus.	Group made decisions by consensus and was able to resolve differences quickly and smoothly.

SCRIPTED

Chapter 3 - Equipment

"You Are Only as Good as the Equipment You Are Using"

The three of us have spent many hours researching and tinkering with the best and most affordable equipment options for our programs. We believe that it is essential to learn everything about operating the audio and video equipment ourselves before we can simplify the process and teach it to our students. Be ready to spend more time than you think when setting up new equipment in your studio or classroom. YouTube is a great resource for equipment and program tutorials. Reach out on social media to other educators using digital media equipment in their classrooms. The best ideas and suggestions usually come from those of us using it every day in the classroom.

When using digital equipment, it is essential to be able to solve the smallest equipment malfunction. Malfunctions can occur at any time. Not all schools have an IT department that can run over at the drop of a hat. It is best to take the time and learn how your studio is set up and how it runs. For example, if a microphone is not working properly, you need to be able to find the source of the problem. Sound issues can be related to multiple sources, so it is imperative to be familiar with all of the equipment the sound is traveling through:

from the microphone, to the soundboard, to the switcher, to the output monitors. It could be one of several potential problems, even as simple as an unplugged cord.

The Big Three

Chapter three provides a breakdown of the "big three." As you will discover, equipment is categorized into three major components: pre-production, studio production, and control room production. We will provide suggestions in each of these areas, based on equipment that we have used or are currently using. Keep in mind, costs may vary based on your supplier of choice. There are several suppliers to choose from. Always check with your district ahead of time for a supplier list or recommendations. Most suppliers offer educational discounts. Due diligence is essential when securing quotes for studio equipment. We all started with the bare minimum; do your research before you make these critical decisions. All the products suggested in this section enhanced our programs and might be wish list items for many school districts. Keep in mind that starting with a device that can record audio and video is all that is needed. Many schools use this model before they add the enhancements outlined in this chapter.

Pre-Production

Pre-production is the planning and creating springboard of your show or production. This is the time when students develop and create the content that is produced for the broadcast. The equipment used during this time is usually very mobile and most likely will be their first exposure to audio/visual equipment. For example, a small digital camera or audio recorder can be easily transported anywhere inside or outside the building to capture images and sound for any type of media project. The better you can explain and model the proper use of equipment, the longer it will last. For example, students who know how to set up a tripod are less likely to break one of the legs when pulling them apart.

Tripods

 There are several models of tripods, typically ranging in price from $50 to $300. One example is the Sony VCT-R640 tripod. It has basic features that students will need, such as panning, tilting, and a steady shot. Many tripods come with the option of wheels, which attach to the bottom of the tripod. It is beneficial to have this capability. The Magnus brand, which has a mid-range price, has been a reliable tripod. There are several models available. When purchasing tripods, keep in mind that students will be carrying these around school, sporting events, and even outside. Purchase a tripod that is sturdy and made to last. The lower-priced tripods usually will only last a few years.

Video Cameras

We've had much success with Canon Cameras in the RF series. The  under $300 cameras use SD cards and have a port to plug in a microphone and headphones. Whatever type of camera you purchase, make sure to check and see that it has a port for audio. The final things you will want to get are external battery chargers and extra batteries for the camera. This will set up the students for success by always having power for the camera. These cameras will be used for capturing images and short video for stories and commercials the students create on their devices.

Microphones

Audio is an essential part of creating great content. The best- produced video will need a strong audio feed. There are numerous microphones to use for every budget. One example is the Audio Technica AT1000 microphones that can plug into small hand-held cameras. We prefer these microphones because the microphone is powered by the camera; there are no batteries. These microphones last a long time. Audio Technica podcasting microphones are great for recording voice-overs on computers. Using an external USB microphone will improve the sound of the project instead of using the built-in microphone on a computer or external device.

Digital Recorders (optional)

Digital recorders are a great way to record sound on the go. They are small and can fit in a student's pocket. Sony digital recorders can record hours of sound, and with the built-in USB, they can upload just as easily as any file. These are easy to grab and use with student projects throughout the year. They are also easily used for student television or radio interviews on location. Digital recorders are a great substitute for recording when plug-in mics are not available or when built-in microphones on devices are not getting the job done. There are several digital recorders on the market ranging in prices to fit every budget and classroom. Digital recorders would be a perfect item for a DonorsChoose.org grant or any other type of funding.

Computers

Computers are a must in pre-production. The classroom should be set up with computers or tablets for students to utilize for pre-production purposes. All content produced is uploaded into the devices where the students use editing video and audio software to create content for the television and radio broadcasts. Work can be saved to external hard drives, LMS, or any cloud-based service.

Television Studio Production

Teleprompter

 A teleprompter is a device that student anchors use to read the script during television production. Teleprompters that use rolling scripts may prove difficult for elementary students. A student must possess fluent reading skills to track a rolling script. PowerPoint or Google Slides work great when teleprompter software is unavailable, or students find tracking a rolling monitor too difficult. Google Slides or Google Docs can make script sharing much easier in the day-to-day schedule.

We use the following brands for our classrooms: Ikan, Prompter People, and MagiCue Studio. Most brands come with software packages.

Green Screen-Chroma Key (color keying)

A green screen provides students with a backdrop when creating digital backgrounds. Green screens also allow students to work on other projects that may require color keying. WeVideo and iMovie, for example, have an easy color keying option that allows the student to take the green screen away from some of their video clips or still shots.

Achieving green screen effects does not have to be costly. For example, a wall can be painted using chroma key paint, or a sheet can be dyed chroma key green. Portable green screens can be purchased for a minimal cost. The green screen can be used for many special effects, which may include ghost heads for Halloween and flying for those superhero shots. It also creates a solid background when shooting still shots. Additionally, green screens make it easy to take out a solid color to create transparent images in the editing process. A green screen can take the students wherever they want with any background.

Lighting

Lighting in a studio is key in making your talent look as good as possible. We all started with the existing lighting in the room. You can purchase lighting kits for the studio, but if you have the budget, it's helpful to have the lights hung from the ceiling or stand-alone light fixtures. It is not necessary to have, but a lighting board will provide the ability to adjust the lights.

Studio Cameras

The number of cameras in a studio depends on the area and the budget. Some cameras, such as Black Magic Design, will also let you control the camera with hardware and software in the control room. This isn't necessary, but if you are starting from scratch, some food for thought, you need to make sure the camera you purchase is compatible with your video-switcher. It's good practice to consult with your IT department before making these purchases.

Microphones

Audio is an essential part of any media you create in the studio. Phantom power microphones do not require batteries and generate power from your soundboard. Hard-wired microphones prevent losing power during a broadcast. Rode and Yeti are two examples of stand microphones used by our anchors during broadcasts.

Lavalier microphones provide the option for mobility during a broadcast. Lavaliers are microphones that can clip on a student's shirt when a hidden microphone needs to be used or if a student has a soft voice.

Television Monitors

You may want to consider installing a couple of television monitors in the studio for preview purposes. This is helpful for students using the green screen during sports and weather segments, so the on-air talent can see the program monitor. Televisions can be mounted on devices such as mobile Peerless TV stands or to a wall.

Furniture and Other Accessories

A green screen is amazing, but sometimes you just need the real thing. If space allows, you can include an area that is not digitally created. For more intimate reports and interviews, you can include a couch and coffee table feel for teachers and students to conduct interviews. The principal, superintendent, or even the gym teacher can produce weekly shows from this space. When large groups of students are being included in the story, this makes a great meeting area. Additionally, securing an anchor desk will add to the professionalism of your show.

Control Room Production

The control room can be as simple as a table and device in any small space. As the studio evolves over time, it's advantageous to find a space where the control room is separated from the studio production area. A large glass window can allow the control room students and teacher to see into the studio, but all the communicating is done through an intercom system. The camera operators, who are in the studio with anchors and reporters, relay all directions to the on-air personalities. The control room consists of the switcher, soundboard, radio equipment, intercom, teleprompter, and computer.

The control room jobs could include Director, Switcher Operator, Producer (communicates all directions through the Intercom system), Soundboard/Audio Operator, and Teleprompter Operator.

Video-Switcher

The video-switcher is the heart of your control room. The video-switcher allows the students to choose what is seen and prepare for what is coming up next in the broadcast. TriCaster and Black Magic are two strong brands of video-switchers being used by our schools. Expect a slight learning curve to master both of these switchers. Utilize program tutorials and make sure multiple students learn how to operate the switcher of choice.

Black Magic

 The Black Magic Design ATEM switcher displays multiple video inputs for students to choose from during broadcast. It also has software to help set up the audio, cameras, and video-switcher. The Black Magic requires a monitor and PC. This particular video-switcher uses SDI in and out connections. Once it's set up, it's an amazing video-switcher.

TriCaster

The TriCaster *"can be utilized in all schools. The Tricaster is offered with several packages."* It offers several camera inputs with multiple effects, including a virtual studio design software. Studios can be created to show off your school logo and even match the seasons. You can also upload student-produced videos and still shots to be used during a broadcast. The TriCaster offers live streaming to your choice of streaming service. Through sites like YouTube Live, parents can tune in from home or wait for the show to be linked to social media or a program website.

Soundboard

It's helpful to have a soundboard to control all the audio for your show. This includes not only the microphones but also audio for music and videos that are played during the show. Make sure the audio board has phantom power. Phantom power is a switch on the audio board that allows power to travel to other devices such as microphones. This will provide power for microphones plugged into the board. It is recommended to purchase a soundboard with as many channels as possible for future program growth.

Control Room Computers

Any platform or computer will work well, but you want to make sure the equipment you are using is compatible with Macintosh or PC. It's important to see what the connection will be between the computer and the video-switcher and the computer and the teleprompter. This might determine your choice of what computer to get, or you can always use the computers you have and make them work with the other hardware in your studio. A computer that inputs into your switcher gives another video input to use as a background. These computers can also be used for supporting the teleprompter, graphics, social media posts, and the script as well. The physical space you have for your control room will determine how many computers you can use.

Headsets/Intercom System

 Headsets are expensive but well worth the investment, if at all possible. One example of headsets is the ComTec wireless system. This system enables all students and teachers to communicate on one channel during a broadcast. The headsets provide students and teachers the opportunity to problem-solve during a live show.

Furniture and Other Accessories

The final consideration is a table, desk, or counter for all studio broadcasting equipment in your control room. There are custom tables, but they tend to be costly. You are going to want to have surge-protected power-on UPS (uninterrupted power source) units to prevent equipment from shutting off during power outages. An affordable UPS unit can save your equipment. It's totally worth the investment. It is also important to have extra wiring, connectors, and adapters in the control room. Sometimes HDMI cables and connections can go bad.

Basic Cables (to keep in stock)

RCA

These cables connect video with the yellow and sound with white and red. These cables are commonly used with older analog equipment. These cables will deliver low-quality audio and video.

XLR

This cable connects to most audio boards for microphones, headsets, and some cameras. All audio boards will have an XLR input for audio. XLR is found on more expensive equipment for better quality.

HDMI

This cable is now common on many flat-panel televisions and monitors. This cable will connect the audio and video. Many newer video cameras will have an HDMI port to connect audio and video.

Splitters (multiple types of splitters needed)

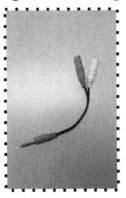

Having extra audio (red and white) and video (yellow) splitters come in handy when connecting to audio boards. The picture is an audio splitter; however, you might need different types of splitters depending on your equipment.

BNC (Bayonet Neill-Concelman)

This cable connects to many of the video-switchers you might use when you begin your studio. For example, many of the TriCaster educational models use this video connection.

equipment you use.

AUX (multiple types of Aux cables and adapters)

It's helpful to ask the IT department as well as the company you are purchasing from what extra cables you might need depending on the

Streaming/Distribution

The last thing to consider is how you are going to broadcast in your school and record the show. You will need to work with your IT department to figure out a solution that works in your school network.

One method of distribution is streaming directly to YouTube. Students and parents can tune into the live show through the YouTube stream during a set school time. Each episode can then be linked to the school Facebook page or website for viewing at a later time. One way to promote your program is to enable push notifications to alert viewers when your show is being broadcast.

Another option is to not stream the show but to record the show live to tape. Once recorded, you will need a plan of how to distribute it, such as YouTube, Twitter, your school website, Google Drive, and other options based on your school capabilities. Many districts block social media sites completely from students, so consider all options before broadcast production.

Radio Studio Production

Microphones

Similar to video production, audio is an essential component in the radio studio. Phantom power microphones do not require batteries and generate power from your soundboard. Hard wired microphones prevent losing power during a broadcast. In addition to Rode and Yeti, the Electro-Voice RE20 Broadcast Announcer Microphone is a cardioid dynamic microphone that delivers reliable, low-noise performance during radio broadcasts. The same microphones can be used for video and audio production. It is not necessary in the beginning to purchase additional sets of microphones.

Headsets

Headsets can be expensive. Invest in good quality sets from the beginning. One recommendation is the Sennheiser HD 280 Pro Circumaural Closed-Back Monitor Headphones, which feature a collapsible design and swiveling earcups. Remember, numerous students will be wearing these throughout the day for extended periods of studio recording and mixing. Invest in good quality headsets. It is also recommended to purchase additional headsets for on-location broadcasts. The headsets enable students to communicate with each other and the teacher during the live production sessions.

Audio Board

It is good to have a soundboard for your radio program as well as your television program. There are several good quality mixers to choose from. The Allen & Heath ZED14 is a good quality unit for the school setting. The Rode RODECaster Pro Podcast Production Studio provides 4 microphone inputs and 8 faders. It is a compact all-in-one unit for all podcast and radio production needs.

Choose the unit which best fits your needs and budget.

Radio Control Room Computers

Any platform or computer will work well, but you want to make sure the software/program you are using for your radio station is compatible with Macintosh or PC. The physical space and type of radio station you have will determine how many computers you will need. Depending on the location of your radio space, you may be able to use the same computer for your video production. As your program evolves, and you acquire additional space, additional computers are options to consider.

Sound Baffle (soundproofing)

 Some radio studios may broadcast from the back of a classroom or even a closet. Consider soundproofing, which will absorb and redirect the acoustics in a room. There are desk-sized as well as full-sized baffles available.

That's a Wrap

Many school-funded programs are on tight budgets when building their radio and television studios, so it's important to start small and add features as your studio grows. You may only need a computer or device with capabilities to record audio and video. As your program expands, revisit your vision and add equipment as needed. Many of us started with just one device that had these functions. There are many low-cost Chromebooks, for example, that have a camera, microphone, and speakers built-in. This might be a logical place to begin.

 **TAKE 1**

> *It is essential to be able to solve the smallest equipment malfunction; know how to operate all of your audio and video equipment.*

 **TAKE 2**

> *Due diligence is essential when securing quotes for studio equipment; do your research before you make these critical decisions.*

TAKE 3

Revisit your studio vision often as you expand your pre-production, studio production, and control room production audio and video needs.

Chapter 4 - Supportive Software

"The Heart of Your Studio"

We have all established strong partnerships and a rapport with supportive software and hardware companies, which have enabled our programs to flourish over the years. One of the most important considerations is customer service, which all three companies below excel at. The companies include WeVideo, a web-based video editing service; Backbone Radio, a web-based Internet radio software company; and Wakelet, a free curation website.

Most of the resources mentioned in this chapter will cost money. All of us have found many ways to generate funds to purchase or offset the cost. The easiest way is to pilot or get a trial to use any software or hardware. Many companies will do this as long as you provide them feedback. WeVideo is an example of one company that provides a free pilot program. While using the hardware and software, showcase student-work in as many places as possible. A presentation by students at a Board of Education meeting or community club meeting goes a long way when looking for future funding. We have found that students can showcase and explain the use of the equipment much better than we can.

When beginning your journey, consider inviting community members, parents, and administrators to join your audio or video broadcast. This provides an opportunity for stakeholders to see your program and your facility. This first-hand look at your program will give them insight into student media innovation.

Who better to tell you about our supportive software than the people who work and own these companies? Here are their stories.

WeVideo - Dr. Nathan Lang-Raad CEO WeVideo

www.wevideo.com

@drlangraad

Who Are We?

Used by millions of students in every grade and subject area, WeVideo empowers every learner to discover their voice and make an impact in their world. Our platform promotes deeper learning while making it fun and easy for students to express their ideas with creativity and authenticity.

In my experience, the most successful learning occurs when teachers are facilitators or activators of learning. Instead of giving formulaic sets of worksheets, tasks, or practice problems, teachers today are designing active, engaging learning experiences that build on student strengths and interests. During these learning experiences, students are empowered to think at a higher cognitive level while creating and engaging with content through real-life problem solving and perseverance.

WeVideo has created an engaging digital playground that supports student-centered learning in the following ways:

- Providing a safe environment for collaboration and research.
- Providing a platform that promotes creativity and innovation.
- Providing a structure for storytelling, reflection, and feedback.
- Emphasizing student voice and a responsibility to share their unique perspectives.
- WeVideo to deepen learning and spawn creativity.

What is the Tool?

WeVideo is a cloud-based comprehensive video creation, production, and management solution built specifically for K-12. Used in over 5000 schools in the US and beyond, WeVideo for Schools is an easy to use, differentiated solution for digital creativity with video, images, graphics, sound, and text. Students as young as kindergarten can easily demonstrate and visualize their learning in powerful and personal ways. WeVideo has worked with many innovative districts that have purchased access for all students, all grades - or in alignment with various 1:1 device initiatives.

WeVideo provides opportunities for deep and highly engaging multimedia creativity for elementary and secondary level students. The application supports (among other things) slideshows, digital storytelling, video creation, and editing, green screen activities, screen recording, explainer videos, voice-over narration, podcasting, audio and music activities, and elements that combine all of the above mixed with animation, text, images and more. Our application includes over 1,00,000 licensed media clips (images, music, videos, sound effects, etc.). This searchable library is built-in, very easy to use, safe for school-age children, and requires no citation or search outside our app. WeVideo supports a broad array of creative opportunities.

To support teachers and staff, WeVideo has built a comprehensive admin section that allows for users to be managed, privacy settings to be controlled, and specific profiles to be created. To facilitate adoption, WeVideo allows admins and tech coaches to create custom templates/lesson plans for virtually any type of multimedia project in any subject area. This lowers the barrier of entry to highly creative activities by making them simpler to set up, taking that burden off the classroom teacher, and making project creation scalable and repeatable (with endless variations).

WeVideo provides opportunities for collaboration, sharing, group projects, and easy integration with widely used education ecosystems (Canvas, Google Classroom, and Drive, etc.).

Instructional Practices

WeVideo supports best instructional practices in the classroom and helps support self-direction and other "success skills" as an integral part of learning. It is this emphasis on critical thinking, collaboration, self-management, and making learning visible that provides even more opportunities for students as they strive toward independence in their post-secondary life. WeVideo connects research around

Constructivist thinking, Bloom's Taxonomy, student-driven learning environments, and meaningful project-based learning experiences. When students use technology tools like WeVideo to scaffold learning, they not only connect more deeply to new content, they interact with content in meaningful ways through inquiry, collaboration, and communication with others within the classroom and outside the classroom. WeVideo supports learning across grade levels, subject areas, and differentiated student needs. It provides a canvas upon which students collect research and drive insights. They are empowered to reveal novel insights they make by establishing connections across content areas.

Video Creation with WeVideo connects to every **ISTE Standard for Students (2016).** Video creation allows students to choose (Empowered Learner) how they will create, researching the internet responsibly (Digital Citizenship). Using the design process (Innovator), students construct new knowledge (Knowledge Creator), building higher levels of thinking complexity through a synthesis of ideas to solve relevant problems (Computational Thinker). Students collaborate (Global Collaborator) with each other and with others across the globe to learn new perspectives. The video creation process provides students with opportunities to communicate clearly (Creative Communicator) and express themselves creatively. *(Cue Card 1: ISTE Standards)*

Our Content

Students are more than a score. The video creation process naturally supports ongoing discovery, reflection, and growth. We believe in supporting students in their learning and growth from beginning to end. Rather than passively consuming media, we believe in actively creating it. We provide tools for students to communicate in effective and compelling ways through video. WeVideo is on a mission to empower students to discover their voice to make an impact in the world. To fully support a student's voice, we must develop the right conditions in which their voices are heard and recognized. Students should be engaged in learning that is both meaningful to them and mirrors the world outside the classroom. With WeVideo, students see how their work impacts their life and those around them. We foster true creativity by balancing open exploration and expression of ideas with support and guidance.

When students engage in such a project, the experience requires more than just acquiring knowledge of a specific content area. It requires inquiry, collaboration, communicating with new people, and the use of technologies that further support student learning.

Formative Assessment

Video creation not only serves as an instructional support and learning experience, but as a powerful and effective formative assessment tool. Video creation overcomes several limitations of traditional assessment. Consider the following reasons:

- Video creation opens the door to organically embracing the revision process without students feeling the drudgery of taking a test.
- Students are motivated to revise their work within a video creation project because the results are instantly viewable and encourage further refinement.

- There is an element of gratification that makes the video creation process more welcoming, especially when juxtaposed with a paper/pencil quiz or test.
- Video creation gives students an outlet for creativity, the output of which the student can feel both proud and invested.

As a formative assessment, video creation illuminates the thinking and learning process, provides opportunities to improve their processes and the product, and reveals misconceptions along the way. Delivering formative assessment through creativity provides students a motivating environment that supports deeper thinking while providing teachers with important data that can be used to inspire subsequent instruction.

Professional Development

If you are interested in getting professional development for your school, then you can ask your administrators to purchase professional development sessions with WeVideo.

- WeVideo 101 for Teachers
- WeVideo 101 for Admins
- Advanced Editing
- Flipped Classroom with WeVideo
- Digital Storytelling
- Hollywood Tips for the Classroom

You can also access WeVideo Academy or the WeVideo Support page or email support@wevideo.com at any time.

🔔Expert Tip

Jennifer Eggert, Instructional Technology Coach, shares tips for tech coaches to help teachers feel comfortable with offering video creation as an option in the curriculum:

1. **Show students examples of all kinds of video projects** (commercials, documentaries, news broadcasts, silent films, etc.). Share a variety of videos that demonstrate differentiated student skills and ability levels.

2. **Share pictures of students** at your school involved in WeVideo Creation.

3. **Encourage teachers to start with it as a choice for students** (think menu, choice boards, etc.).

4. **Direct them to the https://www.wevideo.com/academy and the https://go.wevideo.com/educatorsguide** (be sure to mention the option of Storyboard mode to start). You may even want to create a screencast that the teacher and/or students can play as they work through the steps!

5. **Create a guide for teachers and/or students** to help with production along the way.

6. **Share project and video creation rubrics.**

7. **Co-teach with or observe** another teacher/coach's instruction for the first lesson.

8. **Celebrate the little things**, including difficulties and challenges (they are only temporary).

Backbone Radio - George Capalbo and Richard Cerny

http://backboneradio.com

@BackboneNetwork

Backbone Networks Corporation

Professional Internet Broadcasting for Student Radio Stations

It's been said that college and high school radio was the first educational social network. Today, student-run radio continues to have a key role in communications curricula and extracurricular clubs in schools around the world. Backbone builds stations for schools with technology that is revolutionizing professional radio.

Backbone's Objective

Help schools of all levels to develop productive, fun, and professional sounding student-run Internet radio stations for the benefit of students, families, alumni, and the schools themselves.

Who?

Backbone Networks is a software/service company focused on the development of "cloud-based" broadcast technology, especially Internet radio. While Backbone's client list includes major league sports teams and leagues as well as major market newspapers, Backbone also operates the Intercollegiate Broadcasting System Student Radio Network (IBS-SRN), the largest online network of college and high-school radio stations.

117

Why?

1. *To help students learn verbal communication skills*

Radio has the power to summon the imagination like no visual image can. Consequently, in creating compelling radio programs, students quickly learn skills of using words rather than pictures to engage their listeners. These skills, once learned, will persist throughout their careers and lifetimes. Student-run radio should be the indispensable core of a school's media strategy.

2. *To help students learn technology and job skills*

With the accelerating pace of broadcast and information technology, students have the opportunity to master the interrelationship among today's mix of broadcast technologies, including audio production and recording, streaming, scheduling, and how to use "the Cloud." Participants learn by doing, practicing live on-air broadcasting including remotes, creating and publishing podcasts, launching briefings to smart devices like Alexa®, and maybe even engaging call-in listeners.

3. *To help build a community for students, their families, and their school*

Internet radio, available on phones and hundreds of different devices, can bring together not only club members, but also the families of the entire student body and faculty. Alumni can connect with their schools, no matter where they now live. A vibrant radio presence can also raise your institution's profile among the business community, a potential source of sponsorship.

Where and When?

Like professional radio stations, your student-run station will be on and available 24/7. Sometimes, as your schedules permit, your crew will be on-air live, connected via the Internet to your "transmitter," which resides (virtually) in the cloud. When you finish airing your live programs, your station will automatically switch over to your automation system to play recorded audio, such as archived shows. That means you are never off the air, although your listeners may think you are broadcasting live at that moment, whether at night, on holidays, or over summer vacation. You can update and modify your schedule from anywhere, and your students can broadcast live from anywhere they can get an Internet connection, including overseas.

How? Backbone has raised the bar in radio broadcasting by:

1. Virtualizing in the cloud. This means all of the expensive production hardware has been replaced by software and located where you can manage it and/or broadcast from anywhere. That includes your automation system, PBX, storage, and streaming servers. All you need is a Mac, a mixer, and a couple of microphones, plus an Internet connection.

2. Integrating the many functions of broadcasting into a comprehensive workflow, saving much time and cost. No longer are live streaming, podcasting, and automation separate challenges, but rather part of an intuitive flow in a purposeful system. Students and faculty advisors may now focus on the broadcast content.

3. Sharing your produced content with other IBS member stations, if you desire, to automatically create a peer-to-peer radio network in the cloud. Backbone serves student-run stations with the very same products as its "major league" stations but highly discounted. While some universities require the whole "Production Suite" bundle, most schools simply opt for Backbone Radio and possibly add phones (Talk) later.

The three primary modules include:

1. Backbone Radio™—Complete Internet radio station, including live assist and automation scheduling software, producer and talent software modules, cloud storage library, 2,500+ preloaded songs, streaming, recording, podcast generation/hosting, Alexa feed, station website, and more.

2. Backbone Talk™—Multiline call-in phone system in the cloud, talent and remote/local screener modules, specially designed for demanding talk/news/sports shows.

3. Backbone Co-Host™ —For remote correspondents and guests in studio quality using a smartphone (includes LUCI Global ® service) with unlimited usage and users, also used for multi-location, multi-host collaborative broadcasts.

How Much?

At the time of publication, Backbone Radio is available to schools at a 25% discount to IBS member schools, or $2,700 annually, normally $3,600 (join IBS: $125/year, http://collegebroadcasters.tv/).

Streaming and hosting are included. Your school may also qualify for the flat performance royalty rate to *Sound Exchange* of $500/year, with a $100 non-reporting option.

<u>Wakelet - Misbah Gedal - Head of Partnerships</u>

www.wakelet.com

@wakelet

www.wakelet.com

What is Wakelet?

Wakelet is a free-to-use content curation and collaboration platform that allows people to capture, organize, and share mixed media content through visual, engaging collections. It is used by organizations, businesses, individuals, academic institutions, and educators.

Curation is a timeless and critical skill, one that activates other key skills like creativity, critical thinking, communication, and much more. As a company, being human is at the heart of everything we do. We want to empower educators and students to have a real say in the functionality, features, and design of the platform. This approach has created a unique and passionate community around the platform. Our community stretches across the globe, and we make a point to listen to the needs of educators, gather feedback, and provide the best curation experience possible.

What can you do with Wakelet?

With Wakelet, you can save and embed all kinds of online content into a collection. For example, you can simply copy and paste the address of a YouTube video into Wakelet, and it will embed it into the collection, allowing viewers to watch it without leaving the site. The same applies to social media posts, articles, podcasts, music, and much more. You can also add and upload your own content into collections, like text, PDFs, images, and even Flipgrid videos. We have a wide range of integrations, layouts, and options that allow you to share content and tell stories exactly how you want.

With Wakelet's collaboration feature, you can create memorable and meaningful learning experiences for your students. Without even needing to sign up or register, students can both access and contribute to collections across devices. Educators are using this feature to assign powerful group assignments, crowd-source resources and feedback from their students, and allow them to share fun, human moments with their classmates.

You can also provide templates for other people to use through our copy feature. This allows you to create a collection and allows other people to copy it to their account, so they can build on it and "jump-start" their own creative process.

We are constantly improving the platform, adding new features, and providing useful functionality that makes a real difference to educators, students, and individuals everywhere.

How are Educators using Wakelet?

Educators across the world are using Wakelet in so many powerful and creative ways, including:

- School / classroom newsletters
- Digital research
- Class microsites and resource libraries
- Visual idea / inspiration boards
- Digital storytelling assignments

- Reflection / mood boards
- Collaborative assignments and group projects
- Digital portfolios
- Lesson plans
- Much more

Curation in education is a simple, yet powerful concept. The ability to take lots of different types of media, add your own context and thoughts, and then share them as a visual, engaging collection makes for some truly unique learning experiences.

Wakelet is often described as an EdTech Swiss Army Knife. The platform is responsive, easy to use, and flexible. It's this versatility that allows educators to innovate and constantly come up with new ideas of how they can use it both inside and outside of the classroom. Our integration with Microsoft's Immersive Reader boosts inclusivity and accessibility, allowing collections to be experienced regardless of the viewer's age, reading ability, or language. In order to better fit into educators workflows and enhance learning outcomes, we've integrated with several platforms, including:

- Flipgrid
- Microsoft Teams
- Microsoft OneNote
- Microsoft OneDrive
- Remind
- Google Classroom
- Buncee

How can Educators use Wakelet as a tool for creation?

Educators are creating some amazing collections on Wakelet. There's something really powerful about the ability to combine content from across the web with your own content, leading to endless possibilities. We've focused on making Wakelet as visually engaging as possible - giving you the option to add cover images, background images, text formatting, and layout options in your collections.

It's this element of creativity that makes every Wakelet collection unique. A teacher using Wakelet for classroom newsletters, for example, can design that newsletter however they want. They can add photos of their students' learning, inspirational or instructional YouTube videos, Tweets from proud parents and the school community, video clips of recitals, sports games and events, and much more.

Educators can also create visual, living, breathing resource libraries to help their students learn more effectively. Rather than sharing a list of hyperlinks and URLs, a teacher can create an entire page on Wakelet dedicated to any topic, bringing subjects to life and engaging their students like never before. It's never been easier to create a beautiful looking resource library that captures and holds the attention of students, whilst also having the ability to share your own thoughts, ideas, and instructions. You can, for example, quickly record a video directly into a collection using our Flipgrid integration, explaining why the resources are important, and adding much-needed context.

How can Students use Wakelet as a tool for creation?

Creativity is one of the most exciting and gratifying skills for a student to learn. Wakelet gives students the ability to express themselves in some unique and effective ways. Not every student is a natural creative, and yet through curation, they can achieve the same gratification of creation through organizing content they find on the web as well as their own. Students have been creating journals on Wakelet, completing powerful storytelling assignments, creating digital portfolios, and much more. We've made it as easy as possible for students to create collections that are truly theirs - leading to memorable pieces of work throughout the school year.

Take digital portfolios, for example. Students use Wakelet to collect evidence of their achievements, favorite school moments, and work they are most proud of, creating colorful, human portfolios that showcase their personality and bring their school career to life. Rather than just writing that they are in the school band, they can instead add a YouTube clip of the band performing. If they play on the school basketball team, they can add a video of the game-winning shot they scored, and the reactions on Twitter afterwards. It's all about empowering these students to get creative and tell their own stories.

The same applies to creative storytelling assignments, group projects, and much more. Students can unleash their creativity and use the power of the internet to produce meaningful pieces of work that they can share with their classmates and the wider school community.

Additionally, our Student Ambassador Program gives teachers the opportunity to empower their students to become leaders. Creativity plays an important part in the program, with students using a tool of their choice to create a flag, whilst using Wakelet to explain their thoughts and inspiration behind the design.

Wakelet is a life-time platform, with its functionality being applicable to every stage of life or career. Whether it's through school, higher education, work, or personal life, curation plays an important part in organizing everything from research, assignments, and dissertations, to planning an event, personal bookmarking, and sharing the things you're passionate about.

Professional Development

Teachers across the world have found Wakelet to be the easiest and most effective way to both record and reflect on their professional development. The ability to quickly capture resources, certificates, qualifications, grad credits, and more, make Wakelet the perfect place to keep track of your career.

Whether through a public professional portfolio that showcases your achievements, or private collections filled with resources and material, there's never been a more efficient way of capturing the things you're doing, all in one place. Educators are even using Wakelet to earn graduate credit by providing evidence of their most successful teaching moments, and the impact they've had on their students and learning communities.

That's A Wrap

The companies represented in this chapter offer supportive software, which can assist all educators in establishing their digital podcasts, radio, or television broadcast programs. This chapter has three major components of radio and television software and hardware.

In the next chapter, you will discover an amazing list of online tools to enhance your media projects.

 **TAKE 1**

> *The most successful learning occurs when teachers are facilitators or activators of learning and empower every learner to discover their voice and make an impact in their world.*

 TAKE 2

> *Radio has the power to summon the imagination; students have the opportunity to master the interrelationship among today's mix of broadcast technologies.*

 TAKE 3

Knowledge of networking and general information technology translates into job opportunities in the real world.

CHAPTER 4 CUE CARDS

"Supportive Software"

CUE CARD 1

ISTE Standards and State Standards Examples

Listed below are the ISTE Standards for Students (2016) that we use to drive the curriculum in our mass media classrooms. These standards serve as the backbone of our broadcasting media curriculum.

ISTE Standards: https://www.iste.org/standards/for-students

EMPOWERED LEARNER

Students leverage technology to take an active role in choosing, achieving, and demonstrating competency in their learning goals, informed by the learning sciences.

1b

Students build networks and customize their learning environments in ways that support the learning process.

1c

Students use technology to seek feedback that informs and improves their practice and to demonstrate their learning in a variety of ways.

1d

Students understand the fundamental concepts of technology operations, demonstrate the ability to choose, use, and troubleshoot current technologies, and are able to transfer their knowledge to explore emerging technologies.

DIGITAL CITIZEN

Students recognize the rights, responsibilities, and opportunities of living, learning, and working in an interconnected digital world, and they act and model in ways that are safe, legal, and ethical.

2a

Students cultivate and manage their digital identity and reputation and are aware of the permanence of their actions in the digital world.

2b

Students engage in positive, safe, legal, and ethical behavior when using technology, including social interactions online or when using networked devices.

2c

Students demonstrate an understanding of and respect for the rights and obligations of using and sharing intellectual property.

2d

Students manage their personal data to maintain digital privacy and security and are aware of data-collection technology used to track their navigation online.

CREATIVE COMMUNICATOR

Students communicate clearly and express themselves creatively for a variety of purposes using the platforms, tools, styles, formats, and digital media appropriate to their goals.

6a

Students choose the appropriate platforms and tools for meeting the desired objectives of their creation or communication.

6b

Students create original works or responsibly repurpose or remix digital resources into new creations.

6c

Students communicate complex ideas clearly and effectively by creating or using a variety of digital objects such as visualizations, models, or simulations.

6d

Students publish or present content that customizes the message and medium for their intended audiences.

GLOBAL COMMUNICATOR

Students use digital tools to broaden their perspectives and enrich their learning by collaborating with others and working effectively in teams locally and globally.

7a

Students use digital tools to connect with learners from a variety of backgrounds and cultures, engaging with them in ways that broaden mutual understanding and learning.

7b

Students use collaborative technologies to work with others, including peers, experts, or community members, to examine issues and problems from multiple viewpoints.

7c

Students contribute constructively to project teams, assuming various roles and responsibilities to work effectively toward a common goal.

7d

Students explore local and global issues and use collaborative technologies to work with others to investigate solutions.

ISTE. International Society for Technology in Education, www.iste.org/standards/for-students. Winter 2019.

INDIANA MIDDLE SCHOOL STANDARDS

Example of State Standards

Listed below are the standards for Mass Media and Media Literacy according to the DOE in Indiana for a middle school curriculum. These standards are being used here for illustrative purposes--your state will likely have similar standards. Make sure you refer to the standards for your state, as you build or construct your media program. These standards should be aligned with your instruction, in addition to the ISTE Standards.

SPEAKING AND LISTENING

Guiding Principle

Students listen actively and communicate effectively for a variety of purposes, including for learning, enjoyment, persuasion, and the exchange of information and ideas. Students adjust their use of language to communicate effectively with a variety of audiences and for different purposes.

MEDIA LITERACY

Guiding Principle

Students develop critical thinking about the messages received and created by the media. Students recognize that media are a part of culture and function as agents of socialization and develop an understanding that people use individual skills, beliefs, and experiences to construct meanings from media messages. Students develop media literacy skills to become more informed, reflective, and engaged participants in society.

INDIANA HIGH SCHOOL STANDARDS

Example of State Standards

Listed below are the standards for Mass Media and Media Literacy according to the DOE in Indiana for a high school curriculum.

INDIANA

High School Mass Media and Media Literacy Standards

https://www.doe.in.gov/sites/default/files/standards/mediastandards 1.pdf

Standard 1 - Historical Perspectives

Students define, describe, analyze, and evaluate the development, timeline, and function of mass media to gain a perspective of the pervasive and influential effect of mass communication on modern life around the globe.

Standard 2 - Mass Media and Society

Students analyze and evaluate the communications models that explain the dynamics of mass media, the nature of the transmissions of cultural contexts or climates, and the impact of mass media on individuals and communities in a society that has a free and independent press.

Standard 3 - Governance, Law, and Ethics

Students understand and apply knowledge of government regulations, laws, and ethical principles related to mass communication and the functioning of media in the United States.

Standard 4 - Media Literacy

Students use their comprehension skills, knowledge base, and information from various media sources to develop a broad perspective that enables them to analyze and evaluate the meanings of mass communication messages they encounter.

Standard 5 - Writing About Mass Media

Students write, present, or produce narrative, informational, and persuasive compositions or presentations in response to their analysis and evaluation of media stories and reports. Student writing and presentations demonstrate a command of Standard English and the research, organizational, and process strategies necessary for an effective composition or presentation. Writing and presentations demonstrate critical thinking and an awareness of the intended audience and purpose.

Standard 6 - Research

Students use their research skills to examine, analyze, and evaluate issues and topics that have received coverage in the mass media and that are of importance at the local, state, national, and global levels. Students write research reports or deliver multimedia presentations that use a systematic research process (defines the topic, gathers information, determines credibility, reports findings). They examine the impact of both media convergence and media research on the quality of mass media information.

Standard 7 - Consumers of Mass Media Information

Students study the connection between journalism and civics to help them become knowledgeable consumers of mass media information and prepare for their roles as informed citizens in a democratic society.

Office of Curriculum & Instruction/Indiana Department of Education. "Guidelines for Syllabus Development of Mass Media Course (1084)." *Indiana Department of Education*, Sept. 2008, www.doe.in.gov/sites/default/files/standards/mediastandards1.pdf.

Chapter 5 - Media Toolbox

"Producer vs. Consumer"

The media classroom provides students with opportunities to create, collaborate, and share their classroom content through digital media. Our task, as media instructors, is to model tools of technology to assist students in designing and sharing information globally, confronting and solving problems collaboratively, creating multimedia texts, and managing multiple streams of simultaneous information. The following websites provide students, from the youngest of ages, a chance to become a producer and not just a consumer when creating media.

Organization

As mentioned earlier in the book, the media classroom can be very chaotic at times, but we reference this as organized chaos. One of the challenges is keeping up-to-date with the ever-changing websites, programs, and applications used in the media classroom. Over the years, we've used an array of programs to assist in the creation process. We continue to update our creation library as new technologies emerge. Many of these tools are free or come with free versions. We have contacted many of these resources ourselves to inquire about a free teacher version or a discount for educators. Some of these resources could be created for free with Google Suite, which is free for all schools.

Wakelet (https://wakelet.com) enables teachers, as well as students, to organize content from the web, including images, videos, articles, tweets, and any link that can be found on the web. These collections can then be posted within your class LMS for easy access. (Free)

LucidChart (www.lucidchart.com) is a website that is used with students when storyboarding and diagramming. It helps organize a vision for their video and audio productions. Brainstorming becomes a fun task for all students. Integrating pictures and words into webs and storyboards, the students have the technology to quickly get their ideas written in an organized diagram of choice. There are several templates that students can utilize when they need assistance getting started. (Free)

Google Slides can be utilized in multiple ways in the media classroom. One specific use is for scriptwriting. When writing a script, Google Slides integrates easily into a teleprompter system in a studio. Students can easily write a script and add it to the shared slideshow. When a guest joins the show, they can add their script to the shared show and be able to read it immediately. Google Slides is one of the most important tools that we use when organizing our news broadcasts. Google Slides can be shared with all students, allowing for comments and corrections by all students involved in the production process. (Free)

Editing and Production

Numerous tools can be utilized to create videos. You can choose to use Google tools and a video editing suite or find third party websites and apps that can add to your project. Many times it's helpful to use just a few tools depending on the project. Here are some of those tools:

Google Drive

Drive, Slides, Docs, and Draw

With these four programs, you can organize, plan, share, and write your scripts. When producing products at the various grade levels, you must consider the grade level and the software each grade level can understand and use. For example, a first-grade student might walk in the door on the first day of school, unable to login to the computers. Once the students gain a basic understanding of the keyboard and the toolbars in the programs, they will have an understanding of the production and design programs they will use in later grades. (Cue Card 1: Elementary Flowchart of Google) (Free)

WeVideo (www.wevideo.com) is an online video editor that works hand-in-hand with Google Drive. WeVideo will work on any device, and, in fact, you can start a project on one device and continue on another device. WeVideo can also be your one-stop shopping for video clips, still images, and audio and sound effects that are all copyright free. You can also open up your Google Drive right in your project in WeVideo. (Cue Card 2: WeVideo) (Free or Paid)

iMovie is an application within all Apple devices. This program works on a single device but is very easy and powerful to use. It integrates with other Apple tools such as Garage Band and Photos. iMovie is also an app that works on any iPhone. (Free)

Squared 5 or Mpeg Streamclip

(**http://www.squared5.com**) converts the file size of the file. Squared 5 or Mpeg Streamclip is a great app for converting file size. This app works on both Mac and Windows. (Free)

Lucidpress (**www.lucidpress.com**) is a great visual design program that allows students to convert their creations to JPEGs, PDFs, and PNGs. This program is used to design many visuals for student projects. From cereal box covers to images promoting school events, this program does a great job supporting a student's design idea. (Free or Paid)

Canva (**https://www.canva.com**) is a graphic design program, which provides free stock photos, templates, icons, and editing features. Students can design presentations, digital posters, social media graphics, and more. Canva also provides tutorials on all design options. (Free or Paid)

Pixlr (**www.pixlr.com**) is a website for editing photos. Students can cut, copy, paste, and much more on this free website. (Free)

Flaming Text (**http://www.flamingtext.com/**) and **Text Giraffe** (**https://www.textgiraffe.com/**) are simple sites used for designing FREE logos for your digital media projects. The logos take seconds to design and can be quickly added to your broadcast or website. (Free)

Panzoid (www.panzoid.com) is a background, clipmaker, and video editor program that students use to create interesting intros. Panzoid provides students the opportunity to change the code inside pre-made templates to match the ideas they have in their minds. There is a slight learning curve to this program. (Free)

SnoSites (https://snosites.com/) is an online journalistic publishing site. The websites are preloaded with everything needed to publish your school news. Hosting is provided by the company, and the support staff is undeniably helpful. There is a one-time setup fee and a minimal yearly fee. The site uses WordPress as the platform. The website can be utilized in numerous ways in the classroom, from blogging, news reporting, radio and television streaming, or school newspaper. (Paid)

Audio Production

Soundtrap (www.soundtrap.com) is the website to go to when producing audio projects. Soundtrap offers a student an online music studio to create anything from thirty-second commercials to full radio shows. The online studio offers opportunities for students to collaborate on projects, download their sounds, and even create their songs. Combining multiple tracks at once gives the student audio creation freedom. The students become the music and radio show producer. The audio projects created on this site are easily converted to an MP3 and downloaded for use in other media, such as WeVideo, Backbone Radio, and even the daily news broadcast. (Free and Paid)

The following sources are royalty-free music sites, which host tracks that can be downloaded as MP3s and include creative-common licensing information. The tracks can easily be added to a radio broadcast, video, or podcast. (All Free Below)

1.   Incompetech (https://incompetech.com/)

2.   Zapsplat (https://www.zapsplat.com/)

3.   YouTube Audio Library
(https://www.youtube.com/audiolibrary/music)

4.   DigMixter (http://dig.ccmixter.org/)

5.   FreeSound (https://freesound.org/)

6.   Jamendo (www.jamendo.com)

Publish

Attribution, copyright, public domain, and creative commons are all terms too familiar in the media classroom. Creative Commons (CC) (https://creativecommons.org) is a search site with over 300 million images, all CC licensed. There are several benefits to this site:

a.   The attributions have already been written for students and can easily be embedded into a final video or project.

b.   There is detailed image information provided, including the source and type of license.

c.   The image can be shared immediately to social media sites.

Student work can be published in many ways. Seek out multiple methods for student publication. For example, in first grade, just printing a Google Drawing is a form of publishing. Google Drive has brought a new dimension to publishing. Consider a common television screen in the school, where school announcements, weather, news, etc. could run all day, which is another form of publishing.

Today, the ultimate goal of many students is to publish globally. Social media sites like Twitter, Facebook, and Instagram have redefined what it means to publish in schools today. Students are even starting to publish in real-time with programs like SeeSaw and Canvas. There is no right or wrong way to publish a student's work, as long as the student feels a sense of purpose for their creation.

Lastly, producing a daily television news or radio show offers students the opportunity to publish work for their peers. Students enjoy hearing their voices and seeing their creations over the daily news or the radio. Peer recognition in the school can be a very motivating and rewarding experience for students.

That's a Wrap

As you begin your journey, start with a few tools to create content and add more tools as needed. Be selective in the tools used to create quality student work. Students can be the best teachers when it comes to learning new software and hardware. The more they are immersed in creation technology, the faster they will move from a consumer to producer of quality products.

 **TAKE 1**

The media classroom provides students an opportunity to become producers and not just consumers when creating media.

 TAKE 2

Be selective in the organizational, editing, and production tools used in the digital media classroom; start with a few key programs or applications.

 TAKE 3

Immerse your students in creation technology--they are often the best teachers.

CHAPTER 5 CUE CARDS

"Media Toolbox"

Cue Card 1

Example: Elementary Flowchart

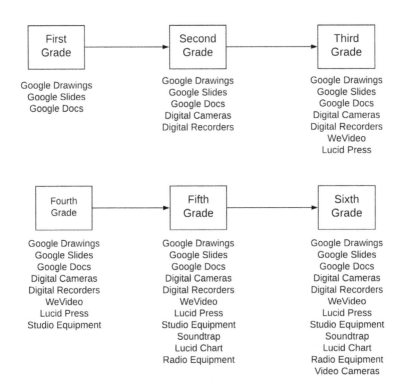

Programs Used in Media Curriculum

First Grade	Second Grade	Third Grade

Google Drawings
Google Slides
Google Docs

Google Drawings
Google Slides
Google Docs
Digital Cameras
Digital Recorders

Google Drawings
Google Slides
Google Docs
Digital Cameras
Digital Recorders
WeVideo
Lucid Press

Fourth Grade	Fifth Grade	Sixth Grade

Google Drawings
Google Slides
Google Docs
Digital Cameras
Digital Recorders
WeVideo
Lucid Press
Studio Equipment

Google Drawings
Google Slides
Google Docs
Digital Cameras
Digital Recorders
WeVideo
Lucid Press
Studio Equipment
Soundtrap
Lucid Chart
Radio Equipment

Google Drawings
Google Slides
Google Docs
Digital Cameras
Digital Recorders
WeVideo
Lucid Press
Studio Equipment
Soundtrap
Lucid Chart
Radio Equipment
Video Cameras

Cue Card 2

WeVideo Cheat Sheet

Copyright Free Search
Thousands of copyright free videos, images, and sounds for students to use in their video creation. No worries about copyright when uploading to YouTube.

Person Media Folder
Upload your own video, images, and sounds straight from your Google Drive. Older students can access their phone media by downloading the Google Drive App to their phone. Use the cloud to upload, the circle to record video, and the microphone to record voice.

Text Options
Insert text over your video. Many options to change font types and put motion text into the project. **(Drag to Video line)**

Audio Options
Insert WeVideo copyright free music and sounds to create mood in the video. Remind students that the audio will set the mood of their project. **(Drag to Audio line)**

Transitions
Insert cool transitions between clips. Keep in mind the more transitions in the project, the longer it will take to finish and upload. Students can sometimes get carried away with these options. **(Drag on Video line between clips)**

Graphics
Moving graphic backgrounds can add a nice effect at the beginning of a video to help the title stand out. **(Drag to the bottom Video line)**

Add Video or Audio Track
This is very important when layering images and audio. Example: putting narration on top of music.

Important Note: To delete a track, hover over the film icon or music notes icon and a garbage can will pop up.

Click on your clip to get editing options. Click on the three lines if options don't pop up.

Clip Editor
Use the clip editor for multiple changes to your clip. Students can transform, animate, change color, color key, and even change the speed. *See options below.*

Important Note: To fade audio click on blue line and add a dot. Grab the last dot and drag it down.

Transform Clip
This will allow the students to rotate, flip, fit, and scale the clip. Some actions can also be changed on the screen at the top right.

Animate Clip
This will allow the students animate the clip. It shows where the object on the screen is at the start and finish. Great zooming effects can be added.

Color Clip
This will allow the students to changed the color hues, tint, saturation, etc. of the clip. It can give some graphics some cool effects.

Color Keying
This will allow the students to use green screen effects and add cloning effects into their videos. It can erase solid colors in each clip. Use the eye dropper to erase colors.

Clip Speed
This will allow the students to change to speed of a video clip. It allows them to put video into slow motion or extra fast motion.

Finishing the Video

When the video is complete, click on Finish at the top of the page. Give the video a title. You have options of how you want to save the video or just audio. Make sure to save the resolution as HD (1280x720). It is also important for students to save it to their Google Drive, so make sure they click on the icon under the destinations. They will have to allow WeVideo to access the first time.

Chapter 6 - Global and Community Impact

"A Global Audience Is Your Future"

Most school broadcasting programs are stand-alone departments, as the three of us can attest. Our three programs were created from scratch. We had no existing programs, and in some cases, no existing studio space or equipment. Each of our programs has evolved by building community awareness and support, creating an authentic global audience, and through communication.

Community Financial Support

We all have embraced the importance of community in our programs and used these resources in a variety of capacities.

Middle School Example

One avenue of community support is through sponsorships. Students learn the basic fundamental marketing aspects of media by producing commercials for various businesses in our community in exchange for monetary sponsorships.

- Students are responsible for contacting the businesses, setting up the commercial shoots, writing the scripts, and filming and producing the final commercials.
- As we are in a smaller community, we can travel to and from the school within forty-five minutes by school bus. Often, we produce the commercials during a class period; however, this isn't always the case. There have been instances in which a small group of students will meet separately at a local business after school to produce not only a commercial, but a feature story as well.
- Some local businesses pay for their sponsorship according to our sponsorship levels, while others donate gift certificates that we use throughout the year for weekly giveaways.
- We focus on businesses in town that are student-friendly, such as bakeries, sweet shops, pizza, and even our local banks.

Several strategies can be implemented to enhance the possibility of gaining funding for your program and building community awareness and support.

1.   One example is sponsoring a community media day or night in which students invite community businesses and leaders to the school, where students showcase their media productions.

2.   Another strategy that we've all used is utilizing community members as mentors within our program. In many cases, the community is unaware of the funding needed to support the media programs in their schools.

3.   Finally, a basic strategy that we used during the infancy of our program was writing and sending introductory letters to potential

community sponsors. Students generated a list of businesses and composed the letters that were sent out.

These are just a few possibilities that can be implemented when seeking funding locally for your program. *(Cue Card 1: Sponsorship levels)*

We have developed a more defined sponsorship with one of the banks in town. They have not only provided monetary support, but they have also provided money for our program shirts, which are designed by students. Designing logos for our program, using Photoshop and other graphic design applications, provides an additional avenue for student-centered learning. Finally, our primary bank sponsor appears weekly on our program with a segment titled, "Money Minute."

In March of 2018, we were asked, with this same local community bank, to produce a sports broadcast simulation, which was used to announce their CSR of the year, during their awards banquet. Students were given information about each candidate and produced a sports broadcast format as a platform to introduce each person. The entire regional bank personnel was in attendance. This provided another avenue for students to build community relationships and add to their authentic audience repertoire.

Lastly, we have been able to secure financial support from several not-for-profit organizations in our community, such as The American Legion and Delta Theta Tau Sorority, both philanthropic organizations. These organizations are sometimes overlooked. Many of these organizations are seeking student programs that require monetary support. In several instances, students have presented an overview of our program at an organization's meeting. This exposure enables students to further their public speaking skills and provides these organizations an opportunity to speak with the students themselves.

Authentic Audiences and Experiences

Middle School Example

One opportunity offered to my middle school media students by our high school athletic department has been the opportunity to announce play-by-play radio broadcasting at both varsity football and basketball games. The best way to learn play-by-play broadcasting is to simply jump in the booth and begin speaking. The football media booth is a learning playing field, as radio outlets from around the area provide mentoring opportunities for the students. We have been fortunate in forming a buddy system with one of our local radio stations. They have taken the students under their wings, by pairing up with the students both on our station and on their local AM/FM station during the games. The opportunity is open to any student in the program who wants to try their voice at play-by-play sports broadcasting.

In addition to sporting events, community festivals and parades also afford broadcasting and interview opportunities for students. Our community hosts one of the largest festivals in the country during Labor Day weekend. We have utilized this event as a vehicle for feature story production for both radio and television. As our radio station is Internet-based (Backbone Radio Network), we can take our radio everywhere. This past year, we produced our entire show from the park, including exclusive interviews and footage. A portion was done during the class period, while additional footage was produced after school. *(Cue Card 2: On-location permission)*

Not only does a Media Night invite community involvement, but it once again drives our goal of authentic audience and global impact. Several years ago, we launched a media night, which provided broadcasting students the opportunity to showcase our program. We secured a Keynote Speaker for the event, which took place in the auditorium. Following the Keynote address, students hosted the night by presenting the various aspects of our program, with examples of shows, commercials, and broadcasts. Following the presentation, parents and community audience members were divided into groups and were led on tours of our studio and other components of our program. We also used this night as an opportunity to reach possible new sponsors for our program. As with all of our programs, the evening is student-driven. *(Cue Card 3: Media Night)*

Radio Day is the newest event that has been incorporated for the last two years. There are designated National Radio Days both at the high school and college levels. There are two scheduled a year--once each semester. The purpose of our Radio Day is to engage the entire school throughout the day. We feature students, teachers, and classes each hour, provide giveaways based on trivia, use our phone system to encourage call-in guests, and invite community members as special guests. Radio Day promotes community involvement and an authentic audience for our broadcasting program. *(Cue Card 4: Radio Day)*

Elementary School Example

Our elementary school is one of eleven in a district of about 16,000 students. Each month the superintendent visits our studio and records his monthly news segment called "Lawrence Live." During this segment, the superintendent interviews students and teachers from around the township while highlighting their accomplishments. Fifth- and sixth-grade students run the studio for these segments. The show is uploaded to the district website and included in the digital newsletter each month. The segments are sometimes picked up by the community television station and run throughout the month. Many community members have an opportunity to see what elementary students can produce.

Career Day in our school also gives our studio a chance to shine. Throughout the day, students interview many adults about their occupations. We have had many distinguished guests in our studio each year, such as Miss Indiana, local radio DJs, and even mayors have come in for interviews with our students. This day provides students an authentic learning experience.

Our authentic audience is our students in the school, as well. Our daily announcements are produced each day and include interviews and school highlights. An email is sent to parents notifying them when their child will be showcased on the announcements. Additionally, we thank them for getting their child to school early for the show and always include a link to the show. The following events are examples of our authentic programming:

- Red Ribbon Week
- Drug Awareness Week
- Read Across America
- Student council candidate videos
- Battle of the Books
- Authors who are visiting the school
- Speakers who are visiting the school
- Public Town Teen Library
- Students Boy Scout and Girl Scout projects
- Spelling Bee
- Geography Bee
- Samsung STEM Challenge Contest
- Torch Run with police
- Daily video feature highlighting faculty and students on community issues

Global Impact

Providing real-world experiences for students is one of the most challenging aspects of today's classroom. The media classroom is a greenhouse for stimuli. It supports a positive environment in which students learn to channel the information, think critically about the messages, and construct their interpretations of the information.

Classroom objectives must be data-driven, which is the reason why students must see the real-world impact not only in their communities, but globally as well. One feature of Backbone Radio Network (Chapter 4), which we feel is beneficial in this aspect, is the audience data feedback they provide to all their stations.

Additionally, apps such as_Revolvermaps.com, are available for your program website. This specific app provides real-time visitor locations through a 3D Globe. Additionally, tools such as Google Analytics provide accurate data for website driven audience accountability.

"Is anyone listening?" Providing authentic audiences for students in broadcasting ranks as one of the most important aspects of the program. In addition to providing data to students, programming your shows is the next important step. Who will be listening? Who will be watching? Does your school have a set time to watch/listen to the shows each day/week? Have you utilized social media outlets to promote your shows? Have you programmed your radio shows multiple times throughout the day? These are all considerations as you target your global audience.

Communication

The key to any successful broadcasting program is establishing a positive school mindset of possibilities. How can all students in your school benefit from a broadcasting program?

Let's think outside of the box, which is exactly what the three of us did, as we were building our programs. We extended learning not only outside the classroom walls but across the United States. One of the most beneficial lessons that we've practiced multiple times over the last three years is the opportunity for our students to speak with each other through classroom Google Hangouts.

Our Story

Through the aid of social media three years ago, I (Paula Neidlinger, @pneid) met Bruce Reicher, @breicher, a media teacher in NJ. Bruce and I have established our programs as Mass Media Sister Schools. During the last two years, we have exchanged student-produced feature ideas, lesson plans, and hosted several Google Hangouts between our classes. Additionally, @Stormradio, part of our @LJHDigitalstorm program, hosted a live call-in show in which Cavallini students called into our talk show during a Google Hangout, which enabled them to speak, listen, and view the entire program. Admittedly, students were a little apprehensive the first time around to provide authentic feedback to strangers. Still, soon, students were genuinely providing beneficial feedback for each other and engaging in meaningful conversations. After spending time getting to know each other and each school, each of our media classes produced a "Welcome to Our School" mini-segment, which appeared on each other's daily announcement program. These segments exposed each of our schools to students from across the country.

Last year, Randy Tomes, @RandallTomes1, an elementary media teacher in Indianapolis, launched his radio station. We decided to use the same format that Bruce and I had been using and provide his students with the opportunity to speak with several of my radio students. Google Hangouts is just one communication vehicle providing the integration of an authentic audience and a positive learning environment for all of our students in our broadcasting classrooms.

Utilizing social media to extend ties around the globe is imperative in providing real-world communication experiences for our students. This cannot be a "one and done" operation. We all continue to build our three programs by providing our students the opportunity to collaborate via Google Hangouts, radio, and television production.

That's a Wrap

Providing students opportunities to engage with community and global organizations is our responsibility, if we are preparing them to be self-directed learners in a media-driven society. Ensuring that students are reaching authentic audiences outside the classroom walls and around the globe will benefit the world in the future.

 TAKE 1

> *Build community support through sponsorships and community awareness.*

 TAKE 2

> *Provide real-world experiences and authentic audiences for students; look for opportunities within your community and globally.*

 TAKE 3

> *Reach beyond the school walls and build a collaborative force of teachers and students, who think critically and are self-directed learners.*

CHAPTER 6 CUE CARDS

"Community and Global Impact"

CUE CARD 1

Sponsorship Example

(Program Name) 2018-19 Sponsorship

Bronze - $100 a year
Silver- $200 a year
Gold- $300 a year
Platinum- $500 a year
Partner-$1000 +

**Our _____ production crew will work closely with each sponsor throughout the production phase of the audio, video, and display advertising process. Thank you for your support and sponsorship of _____.

_____ Yes, I would like to sponsor _____ during the 2018-2019 school year at the:

Bronze level-	$100	_____
Silver level-	$200	_____
Gold Level-	$300	_____
Platinum level-	$500	_____
Partnership-	$1000	_____

(Checks payable to _____)

My Company Name (if applicable): _____

My Contact Name: _____

My Address: _____

My Phone Number: _____

My Email address: _____

(Insert Program Social Media links)

CUE CARD 2

On-location permission slip example

Community On-Location Reporting

(Date)

I am excited to announce that our (Program) students will be on-location in our community once a month throughout the year. We will be traveling by School Corporation Van/Bus to **(Place)** on **(Date)** during _____. Your child will only be traveling during their Mass Media class time.

(Place)

I give my permission for my daughter/son,

_____, to travel by school van/bus to

the _____. I understand that students will leave **(School Name)** at the beginning or their _____ class/respectively. They will return by the end of the period.

Parent's Signature _____

Student Signature _____

This permission slip must be returned by (Time/Day) in order for your child to travel to the (Place).

(Teacher Info)

CUE CARD 3

Media Night

We have provided Media Night component examples below, including the invitation, Media Night Program, outline of the evening, tour rotation, and presenter, and anchor scripts.

Program

(_____) Media Night- (Date)

Tonight's Hashtag: **#medianightmadness**

- **Welcome & Introduction-** (Name/s)

- **Keynote Speaker-** (Name/s)

- **Presentation of the Mass Media programming-** (Name/s)

- **Publicity-** (Name/s)

- **Television Directors-** (Name/s)

- **Radio-** (Name/s)

- **Tour of the Mass Media Programs**

  o Tour Guides will assist small groups to each of our stations. Tours will be based on the letter on your ticket. Tour Guides for the evening: (Names)

  o Tour Rotation

  o Tonight, you're a DJ on _____ Radio

  o You're a TV Star- guest spot on _____TV

- o Social Media- HASHTAG TONIGHT: **#medianightmadness**

- o StopMotion Explosion- Animation in Film Making

- o Say Cheese! Our photographers are ready with their cameras in our Photobooth

- o Refreshments

- **Media Night Highlight Movie & Door Prizes- meet in the auditorium after tours.**

Order of Presentation (Student Guide)

(This is a sample guide; it can be altered as needed)

1. Television Directors *(Name/s)*

a. Introduce yourselves

b. Thank you again for joining us tonight. At the beginning of the program, you had a sneak peek at _____. During the tours tonight, you will have the opportunity to visit our television production studio. We shall be producing a show before your eyes. After the program, you will have the opportunity to see our finished product.

Our editors, (Name/s) will be editing the show throughout the evening. They are our _____TV editors each day. We also would like to acknowledge our Graphic Design artist, (Name/s), who designs our logo transitions throughout our show.

We produce a show three times a week both in the studio and on location throughout the school and our community. We have several students throughout the day to write, create, and produce the various stories for our program. You can find all of our shows on our website under _____.

We look forward to seeing all of you shortly and explaining more about our program.

2. Radio *(Name/s)*

a. Introduce yourselves

b. _____ Radio is an Internet Radio station, which runs 24 hours a day 7 days a week. We are currently one of only a handful of middle school radio stations in the United States.

For four years in a row, we have received awards at the national level as part of the IBS network.

We produce shows throughout the day during all of our classes. We even have the capability for live call-in talk shows. This year, we will not only continue our live sports coverage at _____ events, but we will also be doing our first ever play-by-play broadcast at two of the _____ football games in the new media booth.

Tonight, we are broadcasting live throughout the evening. Each of you will have the opportunity to be a DJ tonight on _____ Radio.

3. Marketing *(Name/s)*

Our videographers will be filming throughout the evening; smile for the cameras! Additionally, make sure you stop by our Stopmotion Explosion Animation booth and check out our first animated film produced by (Name/s). Finally, make sure you stop by our WebMaster booth featuring (Name/s).

Throughout the evening, we will be available to answer any questions you have about Sponsorship. We will be located at the front entrance.

TV STUDIO TOUR

a. Guests sit in chairs (we will seat them on both stages in-studio)

b. Director will begin by thanking everyone for coming and welcoming them to our studio.

Director Script

Thank you for coming tonight. This is the place we do much of our broadcasting, although we also film on location throughout the school. This year, we will be filming out in the community once a month. Next Tuesday will be our first broadcast outside of our studio. We will be interviewing (Name/s) about the (Event) and then travel to the high school and speak with (Name/s) about the (Event).

You will have the opportunity to see how our TriCaster system operates. We were able to purchase this with sponsorship money and through a grant we received last year- (Donation Name)

We'd like to feature all of you at our end of the program video tonight, so we're going to film a show now. We will need at least one of you to volunteer at this time. (Anchor should already be at the desk. Make sure you get at least 1-2 people in each group to be on the show).

Anchor Script

Good evening, and welcome to a special segment of _____ TV. We are live tonight at the _____ Media Night. We have several special guests in the studio. (camera pans across the audience). (Anchor looks at guest and shakes their hand)

I'd like to welcome _____ to our studio. Thank you for being here tonight. What have you enjoyed most about our Media Night *so far? (**You will need to respond based on what the person says-be yourself-respond like you would.**) Tell us at least one thing you learned tonight that you didn't already know about our program or in general. (**Again, respond based on what the person says.**) Thank you again for being part of our show tonight.*

At this point, if time permits, allow for one more guest to be on the show and follow the same basic format. Try to make it fun for the audience. Remind your audience that at the end of the program, they will see their segment.

Radio Tour

The radio tour will take place in the auditorium. During the actual program, we will be broadcasting Live. You will need to start the program and welcome listeners to the event. (This will be streaming live on our website) As we begin the tour, you will need to explain to listeners what events will be taking place throughout the evening.

During the Tour

Student Script

Thank you for coming tonight. We appreciate your support. We are part of _____ Radio. _____ Radio is a 24/7 Internet Radio station. You can find us on our _____ website and/or download the TuneIn app on your phone.

We primarily run our shows each hour of the school day. We broadcast live and have the capability to re-run the shows multiple times throughout the day and evening. Additionally, we produce commercials for our community sponsors.

We are also fortunate to have our phone number; we can conduct live call-in talk shows. Our number is _____.

We are only one of a handful of middle school radio stations in the United States. We have competed at the national level for the last five years through the IBS network and have won in several categories. Tonight, you're going to be our guest on _____ Radio; we are streaming live as we speak.

(Direction: You will be standing up during this presentation. We will want two DJ's and one guest rotating throughout each tour. Try to get as many guests as possible on-air.)

Radio DJ Script

Good evening, and welcome to our special coverage tonight of the _____ Media Night. We have several special guests on hand.

I'd like to welcome _____ to Media Night. Thank you for being here tonight. What have you enjoyed most about our Media Night so far? **(You will need to respond based on what the person says--be yourself--respond like you would.)** *Tell us at least one thing you learned tonight that you didn't already know about our program or in general.* **(Again, respond based on what the person says.)** *Thank you again for being part of our show tonight. Rotate and get as many guests as possible on the show. (Feel free to add additional questions based on your preparation ahead of time.)*

Invitation

Date:

Dear _____,

You are cordially invited to attend our _____ Media Night on
(date/time) in the _____ auditorium. The evening will kick off
with our Keynote Speaker, _____.

The _____ Media Staff will be presenting and demonstrating some
of the significant technological opportunities available at _____
within the Mass Media program. _____ students will be presenting
and demonstrating exciting programming initiatives within the
_____ program. Additionally, attendees will be participating in live
_____ TV and Radio productions.

We look forward to seeing you on date/time. The program will
begin at _____. It is sure to be an evening consumed with
energetic, creative, dedicated students, who display initiative and
genuine enthusiasm for their education. Thank you for your
support of the _____ program.

Sincerely,

CUE CARD 4

Radio Day

Radio Day possibilities are endless. The format should be student-driven and planned well in advance. Planning to minimize the chance of making mistakes is critical for anyone using the media. The purpose of the event is to generate school-wide student and teacher engagement. Promote your Radio Day through multiple mediums in advance. During the day, post events on social media and your website blog. Be sure to program your music, commercials, tags, etc. well in advance, too. Begin with one day a year and increase as your program expands. Listed below are a few activity ideas that can be implemented during Radio Day:

- *Provide hourly giveaways using trivia questions: questions should be organized and written in advance*
- *Stimulate on-air conversations through academic questions or debate, which have been provided by teachers in advance or students in advance*
- *Invite students to call in with music requests or use your program website or blog to accept requests throughout the day*
- *Secure community guests throughout the day*
- *Invite administration to speak about school or community issues*
- *Raise awareness or money for a school cause or community charity*
- *Include a vinyl segment during day*
- *Include theme shows and class contests where a "Golden Record" can be displayed for the winning class*

Chapter 7

"That's A Wrap"

A digital media curriculum successfully addresses the future workplace skills created by the World Economic Forum. We have identified below the media student-objectives, which meet or address these skills.

Top 10 skills in 2020 according to *The World Economic Forum*

1. **Complex problem solving**--planning, brainstorming, writing and producing a digital project

2. **Critical thinking**--researching complex world, community and local topics and news stories

3. **Creativity**-- presenting, creating, and producing media in an original format

4. **People management**--student leadership within audio and video production

5. **Coordinating with others**--collaborating, producing, and writing content

6. Emotional intelligence--supporting and validating video and audio successes

7. Judgment and decision making--student directors leading students in production

8. Service orientation--creating Public Service Announcements for community organizations and businesses

9. Negotiation--students discussing audio and video content

10. Cognitive flexibility--coordinating student roles and content in all learning environments

Top 10 skills

in 2020		in 2015	
1.	Complex Problem Solving	1.	Complex Problem Solving
2.	Critical Thinking	2.	Coordinating with Others
3.	Creativity	3.	People Management
4.	People Management	4.	Critical Thinking
5.	Coordinating with Others	5.	Negotiation
6.	Emotional Intelligence	6.	Quality Control
7.	Judgment and Decision Making	7.	Service Orientation
8.	Service Orientation	8.	Judgment and Decision Making
9.	Negotiation	9.	Active Listening
10.	Cognitive Flexibility	10.	Creativity

Source: Future of Jobs Report, World Economic Forum

The Big Take-Aways

There is no one "studio-in-a-box" for building a digital media and broadcasting program. The vision for your program will take shape through unified decision making by all stakeholders. Leave no rock or stone unturned, as your decisions on funding, studio space, structure, and scheduling lead you toward your vision.

Embrace a vision for your curriculum; there's more than one path. Create digital media opportunities to perpetuate student curiosities. Integrate and promote creative thinking …*media literacy empowers critical thinking.*

It is essential to be able to solve the smallest equipment malfunction; know how to operate all of your audio and video equipment. Due diligence is essential when securing quotes for studio equipment; do your research before you make these critical decisions. Revisit your studio vision often as you expand your pre-production, studio production, and control room production audio and video needs…...*you are only as good as the equipment you are using.*

The most successful learning occurs when teachers are facilitators or activators of learning and empower every learner to discover their voice and make an impact in their world. Radio has the power to summon the imagination; students have the opportunity to master the interrelationship among today's mix of broadcast technologies. Knowledge of networking and general information technology translates into job opportunities in the real world…*the heart of your studio.*

The media classroom provides students an opportunity to become producers and not just consumers when creating media. Be selective in the organizational, editing, and production tools used in the digital media classroom; start with a few key programs or applications. Immerse your students in creation technology--they are your best teachers...*producer versus consumer.*

Build community support through sponsorships and community awareness. Provide real-world experiences and authentic audiences for students; look for opportunities within your community and globally. Reach beyond the school walls and build a collaborative force of teachers and students who think critically and are self-directed learners...*a global audience is your future.*

Enjoy your journey!

For updated information, go to our website at

www.scriptededucators.com.

<u>Social Media links:</u>

Facebook - www.facebook.com/ScriptedEducators

Twitter -@scriptededu www.twitter.com/scriptededu

Gmail - scriptededucators@gmail.com

Instagram - https://www.instagram.com/scriptededu/

Wakelet - www.wakelet.com/@scriptededu

YouTube Channel - Scripted Educators

Scripted Educators on LinkedIn

Glossary of Basic Broadcasting Vocabulary

Anchor: The newscaster who hosts the studio portion of the newscast. The anchor is the dominant voice in the presentation of the news to the audience. They must be proficient in writing, producing, and editing the news.

Back timing: A convenient way of counting down the length of a newscast. This tells you when each story must run in order for your newscast to end on time.

Break: A place designated within broadcast programming during which commercials run.

Bumpers: Small teases (with or without audio/video) that come at the end of one newscast segment often previewing what is coming up in the rest of the newscast.

Cold Copy: AKA; Rip-n-Read – A script not seen by an announcer until the moment she/he reads it.

Control Room: Where the technical equipment for putting a newscast on the air is kept and operated.

Cue: Usually a physical signal by an engineer or other technical person indicating to anchor to perform a task (start reading, wrap up, or go to break).

Cue Up: Placing a sound bite, package, wrap, voice-over, or other recorded material at its beginning.

Dub: Make a recording of a recording.

Edit: Condense or revise material or footage.

Engineer: Technical personnel who can both operate, maintain, and repair equipment.

Feed: A live or recorded report, or a set of recorded reports sent to a station/newsroom via satellite, phone, or other device for inclusion in a news program.

Feedback: An ear-splitting squeal or howl caused when sound from a loudspeaker is picked up by a microphone and re-amplified.

"Happy Talk": The casual banter that goes on between news anchors and other "on-air" people.

Headlines: A kind of "tease" read at the beginning of a newscast.

Kicker: An offbeat or humorous story that typically is used to mark the end of the news segment and the beginning of the sports/weather segment. The kicker can also be used to end a newscast.

Lead-in: A broadcasting term for the beginning part of story news anchor reads introducing the story and/or person reporting story.

Lead story (aka Lead): The first story in a newscast or segment (in broadcasting) or a story that is above the fold in print-this considered the most important news story of the day.

Live shot/Live Report: A TV news story during which a news anchor or reporter is live at a remote location. Within this report can be included a SOT, VO/SOT, or PKG.

Natural Sound: AKA Nat Sound, Nat S-O-T, or Ambient Sound – Background voices, music, machinery, waterfalls, and other environmental sounds that are recorded on-scene and used to create a sound bed for a recorded or live report. Primarily used for setting a mood or providing atmosphere for a report. This technique is frequently overused, but when used properly, it adds immeasurably to a story.

Out cue: Usually the last thing a reporter says in either a live or recorded news story indicating the piece is ending. (Example: "FOR UPDATE NEWS, I'M BILL SMITH.")

Outro: Usually the "Goodbye" or end segment of a newscast often during which news and sports anchors engage in "happy talk."

P-S-A: AKA Public Service Announcement – An advertisement for a not-for-profit organization, such as the American Heart Association and Partnership for a Drug-Free America.

Rundown: AKA lineup – A chronological outline or order of stories or segments to be used in a newscast. This is the producer's blueprint for the newscast.

Sound bite (SOT): An edited slice of a newsmaker speaking. Similar to actuality in radio except the person can be seen. Often several SOT can be spliced together with the edits covered with video. These can be included in PKGs and VO/SOTs or can stand alone.

Spot News: An unexpected event that can be covered in various ways.

Stand-up: Part of package with reporter on-screen reading/presenting information.

Story Tag: Closing to a story, live shot, or on-set piece usually read by the story reporter but can also be read by an anchor.

Tag: A paragraph at the end of a news story, usually delivered by the anchor, that provides additional information or sums up the item.

Voice-over (VO): A TV news story during which a news anchor or reporter reads a script live as video is played.

Glossary of Advanced Broadcasting Vocabulary

A-Roll: The main portion of audio/video footage in a news story.

Attribution: The written phrase that identifies the source of a fact, opinion, or quote in a story.

Backgrounder: A story used to provide history and context to a current news story.

Beats: The areas of expertise that a journalist or reporter covers regularly and on an in-depth level, such as politics, health, or law enforcement.

Beat Checks: A list of established contacts that a beat reporter will frequently touch base to find or develop a story. These could include the local law enforcement agency, city council, hospital, or other sources.

Blind Interview: More common in print than in broadcast journalism, a blind or off-the-record interview is one in which the interviewee is intentionally left unaccredited (also known as a non-attributable).

Bridge: An audio track linking between two news items.

Chyron: The words on the screen that identify speakers, locations, or story subjects. Chyron is a trade name for a type of character generator.

Closed-Ended Question: A direct question intended to elicit a yes-or-no answer as opposed to an open-ended question intended to encourage a lengthy answer.

Correspondent: A reporter who files stories from outside the newsroom—usually someone assigned to cover events in another city, state, or country.

Crawl: AKA the news ticker, a thin bar of scrolling text which informs viewers of any upcoming breaking news or weather alerts.

Donut: A produced news package with a live shot with a live intro and tag.

Feature: A non-breaking news story on people, trends, or issues. A feature story isn't necessarily related to a current event.

Follow-Up: A story updating or supplying additional details about an event that's been previously covered.

Hard News: The news of the day. Factual coverage of serious, timely events (crime, war, business, politics, etc.)

Hot or Overmodulated: Either too loud (hot audio) or too bright (hot video). Engineers often say that hot video "blooms" on screen.

Hot Roll: When a crew in the field doesn't have enough time to feed back footage to the newsroom, they must roll it live from the truck during the broadcast.

Human Interest: A news story focusing on a personality or individual's story with wide appeal to a general audience.

Join in Progress (JIP): A direction to the control room to cut to a broadcast already in progress.

Lead: The key information of the story, usually presented at the beginning of the segment. Not to be confused with the "lead story," being the first presented in the broadcast and often the highest in priority (confusingly also referred to as the "lead.")

Leading Questions: Questions intended to steer an interviewee in a particular direction.

Lip Flap: Video of somebody talking, with the audio portion muted. Happens when using video of people being interviewed as B-roll. Avoid it.

Live: Put on the air in real-time, not pre-recorded or pre-produced.

Miscue: An error in which footage or audio is played before its intended time, resulting in overlapping elements in the broadcast.

MOS: An acronym for "man-on-street" interview, in which a reporter on location gets spontaneous sound bites composed of reactions to a story from members of the public.

NATSOT or NAT Package: A type of pre-produced package that has no reporter track; the only audio is the natural sound of the video being shown. It may also use interview sound bites. Often used to convey the mood or atmosphere at a scene or an event.

NAT Sound: Natural sound on video that the microphone picks up. Example: Including sound of a rally with video of a rally.

Open-Ended Question: A question phrased in a way that encourages a source to give a lengthy, in-depth answer—as opposed to a closed-ended question, designed to elicit a yes/no answer.

Package (sometimes Wrap): A pre-recorded, pre-produced news story, usually by a reporter, with track, sound, B-roll, and possibly a stand-up.

Production Element: Any piece of audio which is intended for use within the final mix, i.e., jingles, music, sound effects, and other station-specific audio.

Promo: Promotional announcement. In effect, an advertisement for a program a station or channel is carrying.

Pronouncer: Phonetic spelling of a word in a story, placed in copy behind correctly spelled word.

Raw Video: Unedited video, just as it was shot. Also called field video.

Reader: A script read entirely by the anchor on camera, without sound bites or video.

Remote: A live shot from the field, where a satellite truck is required to transmit the image.

Sidebar: A small story, graphic, or chart accompanying a bigger story on the same topic.

Slug: The name given to a story for newsroom use.

SOT or Sound Bite: "Sound on Tape." A recorded comment, usually audio and video, from a news source other than the anchor, narration, or voiceover, played during a news story—usually an edited portion of a larger statement.

Stacking: Lining up stories within a newscast based on their importance and relationship to one another.

Still: A still image as opposed to a moving video image. Stills can be used to illustrate a story and can sometimes be displayed over track or interview clips instead of video footage.

Sting: A brief piece of music, typically less than fifteen seconds, used to punctuate the end of a segment or story. The sting is often the station's own jingle.

Stop Set: The time allotted to any commercial breaks within the broadcast.

Survey Week, Sweeps Week: The week in which a station's viewership is monitored and rated.

Switch: An instruction given to the control room to cut to another camera or video source.

Tag: A paragraph at the end of a news story, usually delivered by the anchor, that provides additional information or sums up the item.

Tease: A short description of an upcoming story designed to keep the viewer watching through commercial breaks.

Toss: When an anchor or reporter turns over a portion of the show to another anchor or reporter.

Track: The reporter's written and recorded script in a news package.

TRT: "Total running time." The length of an edited package.

Upcut: Chopping off the beginning of the audio or video of a shot or video story. Opposite of downcut.

Video Journalist or VJ: A reporter who shoots his or her own video and may even edit it. Also referred to as a "Multimedia Journalist."

Videographer: A name for a photographer or cameraperson.

VO or Voiceover: "Voiceover" followed by "sound on tape." A news script, usually read live, that includes video, track, and at least one sound bite.

Watermark: A semi-transparent graphic, usually the station's logo, placed in one corner of the broadcast feed.

Woodshedding: The practice of annotating a news script to denote which words should be spoken with emphasis.

Glossary of Beginning Film Production Vocabulary

Art Director: The person responsible for the look and feel of the film's set; responsible for set construction, design and props (number, type, and placement).

Aside: When a film character breaks the imaginary "fourth wall" and speaks directly to the film viewers.

B-Movie: A low-budget, second-tier movie, often the second movie in a double-feature billing. B-films were cheaper for studios because they did not involve the most highly paid actors or costly sets.

Background Artist: Also known as a matte artist; the person responsible for designing a visual backdrop to fill in the background of a film scene. Historically created using traditional paints, backdrops today are mostly created digitally.

Backlot: A large, undeveloped area on studio property used for constructing large open-air sets.

Cinematographer: A person with expertise in the art of capturing images either electronically or on film stock through the application of visual recording devices and the selection and arrangement of lighting. The chief cinematographer for a movie is called the director of photography.

Clapboard: Also known as the clapper. A small board which holds information identifying a shot. It is filmed at the beginning of a take. Also called a slate or "sticks."

Direct Sound: When sound and image are recorded at the same time.

Director: The principal creative artist on a movie set. A director is usually (but not always) the driving artistic source behind the filming process, and communicates to actors the way that he/she would like a particular scene played.

Dunning: Combining studio-filmed shots with background footage that has been filmed in a different place.

Executive Producer: Person in charge of production. Not involved in technical aspects, but oversees overall production. Usually involved in the business/finance end of filmmaking. The role of the Executive Producer is to oversee the work of the producer on behalf of the studio, the financiers, or the distributors. They will ensure the film is completed on time, within budget, and to agreed artistic and technical standards.

Eyeline Match: Creating the illusion of a character looking at an object by cutting between two shots.

Foley: The art of recreating incidental sound effects (such as footsteps) in synchronization with the visual component of a movie.

Fourth Wall: The imaginary plane that separates the characters and action of the film from the viewing audience.

Gaffer: Chief lighting technician who is responsible for designing and creating a lighting plan.

Grip: The person responsible for the set-up, adjustment, and maintenance of production equipment on the set.

Head-On-Shot: When the film's action moves directly toward the camera.

Into Frame: A person or object moving into the picture without the camera moving. This is similar to a character making his way onto the stage in a play.

Montage: Editing a sequence of shots or scenes together in a continuous sequence to more quickly convey information over a period of time.

Point of View (POV): A shot from the vantage of the eyes of a character to show the viewer what the character is seeing.

Producer: One or more producers are responsible for seeing a film through from development to production to post-production to distribution. Producers are involved in raising funds, hiring key personnel, and attracting distributors.

Rigger: Workers responsible for setting up lighting and scaffolding on film sets.

Screenwriter: A person who either adapts stories or writes screenplays for film.

Soft Focus: A visual effect blurring the image by using filters or shooting with an out-of-focus lens.

Soundstage: A large area (usually in a studio) where elaborate sets may be constructed.

Stock Shot: Previously recorded footage, such as footage of historical events, which can be edited into the film.

Glossary of Shot Composition and Camera Angles Vocabulary

Arc Shot: In this shot, the camera moves around the object in a circular motion in order to show the image from more angles.

Close Up Shot: This shot tightly frames a person or object to show detail or emotion. The camera will be close to the subject. Close-up panels might focus on a single person's face, a license plate number, or something similar. A Close Up shot includes a medium close up, close up, and extreme close up.

Dissolve: Similar to fades, but instead of going to and from black, one image fades and slowly becomes an entirely different one. (This can be done through editing)

Establishing Shot: This shot sets up the setting of a scene. It is typically at the beginning of a movie or scene.

Fade (fade in, fade out): In a fade out, the subject of the shot slowly fades away until the image is completely black. For a fade in, a black image brightens until we can see what's going on. (This can be done through editing)

Frisbee Shot: This shot places a camera behind (or even attached to) an object that is being carried around.

Head-On Shot: This shot happens when the action comes straight into the camera.

High Angle Shot: In this shot, the camera is located above the subject and films down on it. It is sometimes used to show which character is more powerful.

Insider Shot: This shot takes place when the camera is placed inside an object. It gives a fresh perspective.

Jaws Shot: This shot happens by zooming in while moving the camera backward. It is used to show shocking realization or for dramatic effect.

Jump Cut: Each panel should logically connect to the next one in a storyboard, but sometimes you might want to intentionally create an abrupt transition to highlight a joke or convey something unexpected. These kinds of transitions are called jump cuts because they often make movements seem jerky and disconnected.

Long Shot: This shot shows the entire figure/object in relation to its surroundings. This is typically filmed "far" from the object. The camera is far away from the subject. Maybe you want to convey someone's isolation by showing them walk through an empty field in the distance or show how small they are next to a skyscraper. This shot can be referred to as a long shot, full shot, wide shot, or even an establishing shot.

Linking Shot: This shot tells two stories by showing two different subjects in one shot.

Low Angle Shot: In this shot, the camera is located below the subject and films up on it, usually from the knees up. It can also show the power of a character in a conversation.

Medium Shot: This shot shows the subject(s) from the waist or knees up. It is used to show more body language and less specific detail. The camera is an average distance away. Perhaps two people are eating a meal at a restaurant and the panel is centered on their table.

Pan or Tilt: These words indicate that the camera is turning left to right or up and down within the shot.

Point of View (POV) Shot: This shot shows the scene from a character's perspective. You see through the character's eyes. You might consider incorporating an over-the-shoulder shot when filming a POV shot.

Reaction Shot: Generally used when you have an image of someone simply listening to another person speak.

Reverse Angle Shot: This shot switches between two or more subjects in a dialogue scene. It is shot from the other side of the subject.

Swish Pan Shot: This shot in filming moves the camera from one subject to another very quickly.

Tracking Shot: This shot in filming follows the action at a constant distance. The camera person moves as the subject moves, keeping the subject on-screen at all times.

Zoom Shot: This shot in filming is done by zooming in to isolate the subject or zooming out to show the subject in a wider context.

Glossary of Radio Broadcasting Vocabulary

Aircheck: A demonstration recording by an announcer to showcase their talent. It is also used to refer to off-the-air recordings of broadcasts.

Acoustics: How clearly the sound can be heard in a room; the quality of sound in a given area.

Ad-libbing: Spoken in one's own words, without a given script.

Airwaves: The medium through which radio or television signals are transmitted.

Board: The console that is used for controlling the audio mix and output during a live broadcast or studio-recorded music.

Broadcast: A presentation of a recorded or live program on the radio.

Bumper: A song, music, or another element that signals a transition to or from commercial breaks. Bumper music is an example.

Call Sign/Call Letters: The unique designation of a broadcast station.

Copy: Written material that will be read by a DJ.

DJ or Disk Jockey: A radio announcer who plays music on air.

Drive Time: The rush-hour commuter periods when radio stations usually have their largest audience.

F.C.C.: The Federal Communications Commission is the federal agency that is responsible for issuing licenses, rules, and regulations overseeing all radio-telephone and television originated signals.

Format: The program element; Country, Jazz, Rock, etc.

Morning Drive (AM Drive): Monday through Friday from 5:30 AM to 10AM.

Playlist: The list of songs that a station will play.

Podcast: An audio file, created in the form of a radio show, in which listeners can subscribe to it, so it is automatically downloaded and delivered to a personal audio device.

PM Drive (Afternoon Drive): Monday through Friday from 3-7PM.

Promo: An announcement, live or pre-recorded, promoting upcoming events.

Public Service Announcement (PSA): An ad that is run in the public interest.

Remote: A broadcast that originates live on location, outside the station's studio.

Share: The number of persons who listened to the station during a given time period, expressed as a percent.

Sound Byte: A snippet of audio from an interview that is used in conjunction with a news story. Its length may vary anywhere from :05 to :15 seconds.

Sports Broadcasting: The broadcast, usually live, of a sporting event.

Sweeper: A recorded element, such as a voice, voice-over music, or sound effects, that creates a transition from commercials back to music.

Tag: A short addition, which is added to a radio or television commercial message.

Voice Track: A pre-recorded voice of a radio personality that is recorded and stored in a computer to be played at a specific time.

Bibliography

ISTE STANDARDS FOR STUDENTS. (2016). Retrieved from https://www.iste.org/standards/for-students

Office of Curriculum & Instruction/Indiana Department of Education. "Guidelines for Syllabus Development of Mass Media Course (1084)." Indiana Department of Education, Sept. 2008, www.doe.in.gov/sites/default/files/standards/mediastandards1.pdf.

9 781970 133882